1994

Key
Management
Ratios

Key
Management
Ratios

How to Analyse, Compare
and Control the Figures that
Drive Company Value

CIARAN WALSH

FINANCIAL TIMES
PITMAN PUBLISHING

Pitman Publishing
128 Long Acre, London WC2E 9AN

A Division of Longman Group UK Limited

First published in 1993

Reprinted 1993 (twice)

A CIP catalogue record for this book
can be obtained from the British Library

ISBN 0 273 03957 1

Typeset by PanSet Arts, Maidstone, Kent
Printed and bound in Great Britain by
Biddles Ltd, Guildford and King's Lynn

CONTENTS

To our grandchildren:

Rebecca
Isobel
Benjamin
Eleanor

ACKNOWLEDGMENTS

I wish to express my deep gratitude to those who helped to bring about this publication. To David Crosby of Pitman Publishing, who originated the concept and carried it through. To my friends and colleagues: John O'Sullivan, who is an unequalled source of reference on even the most esoteric subjects; John Dinan, who re-started the motor following a 'blow-out'; and Ray Fitzgerald for his expertise and knowledge of all the finer points in accounting.

I would also like to thank the executives of the Irish Management Institute, Maurice O'Grady and Dorrie Mitchell for their generous provision of facilities and Charles Carroll for helping with space in the timetable.

I am grateful to the staffs of the Irish Management Institute Library and Dublin Central Library, for their unstinted provision of all the financial data that I sought, including data from the *Financial Times* and Extel Financial Ltd; to Geraldine McDonnell, who cheerfully coped with all the work of the section while the author was in seclusion, to the Secretaries of the FT-SE companies – whose departments supplied copies of their beautifully produced published accounts – and to Sally Green and Michelle Clarke for their expert editing.

Finally I would like to recognise the technical excellence of the software and hardware used to produce the manuscript, Ventura Publishing, Lotus Freelance Graphics, Borland Quattro spreadsheet and Dell computers.

Part I

FOUNDATIONS

1 BACKGROUND

'And all I ask is a tall ship
And a star to steer her by.'
John Masefield

WHY DO YOU NEED THIS BOOK?

Business ratios are the guiding stars for the management of enterprises; they provide their targets and standards. They are helpful to managers in directing them towards the most beneficial long-term strategies as well as towards effective short-term decision making.

Also conditions in any business operation change day by day and, in this dynamic situation, the ratios inform management about the most important issues requiring their immediate attention. By definition the ratios show the connections that exist between different parts of the business. They highlight the important interrelationships and the need for a proper balance between departments. A knowledge of the main ratios, therefore, will enable managers of different functions to work more easily together towards overall business objectives.

The common language of business is finance. Therefore, the most important ratios are those that are financially based. The manager will, of course, understand that the financial numbers are only a *reflection* of what is actually happening and that it is the *reality* not the ratios that must be managed.

THE FORM AND LOGIC

This book is different to the majority of business books. You will see where the difference lies if you flip through the pages. It is not so much a text as a series of lectures captured in print – a major advantage of a good lecture being the visual supports.

It is difficult and tedious to try to absorb a complex subject by reading straight text only because too much concentration is required and too great a load is placed on the memory. Indeed, it takes great perseverance to continue on to the end of a substantial text. It also takes a lot of time and time is the one thing that busy managers do not have in quantity.

Diagrams and illustrations, on the other hand, add great power, enhancing both understanding and retention. They lighten the load and speed up progress. Furthermore, there is an elegance and form to this subject that can only be revealed by using powerful illustrations.

Managers operating in today's ever more complex world have to absorb more and more of its rules. They must absorb a lot of information quickly. They need effective methods of communication. This is the logic behind the layout of this book.

METHOD

There are many, many business ratios and each book on the subject gives a different set – or, at least, they *look* different.

We see a multitude of names, expressions and definitions, a myriad of financial terms and relationships, and this is bewildering. Many who make an attempt to find their way through the maze give up in despair.

The approach taken in this book, is to ignore many ratios initially in order to concentrate on the few that are vital. These few, perhaps 20 in all, will be examined in depth. The reason for their importance, their method of calculation, the standards we should expect from them and, finally, their interrelationships will be explored. To use the analogy of the construction of a building, the steel frame will be put in place, the heavy beams will be hoisted into position and securely bolted together and, only when this powerful skeleton is secure, will we even think about adding those extra rooms that might be useful. It is easy to bolt on as many subsidiary ratios as we wish once we have this very solid base.

The subject is noted for the multitude of qualifications and exceptions to almost every rule. It is these that cause confusion, even though, quite often, they are unimportant to the manager. (They are there because they have an accounting or legal importance.) Here, the main part of the book ignores most of these, but the ones that matter are mentioned in the appendices. Many statements will be made that are 95 per cent true – the 5 per cent that is left unsaid being of importance only to the specialist.

THE PHILOSOPHY

All commercial enterprises use money as a raw material which they must pay for. Accordingly, they have to earn a return sufficient to meet these payments. Enterprises that *continue* to earn a return sufficient to pay the market rate for funds usually prosper. Those enterprises that fail over a considerable period to meet this going market rate usually do not survive – at least in the same form and under the same ownership.

This golden rule cannot be overemphasised and an understanding of its implications is vital to successful commercial operations. This is true for individual managers as well as for whole communities.

EXCITEMENT

Not only is this subject important for the promotion of the economic well-being of individuals and society, it is also exciting – it has almost become the greatest sport. Business provides all the thrills and excitement that competitive humankind craves. The proof of this is that the thrusts and counter-thrusts of the entrepreneurs provide the headlines in our daily press.

This book will link the return on financial resources into day-to-day operating parameters of the business. It will give these skills to managers from all backgrounds. The objective is that all the functions of production, marketing, distribution and so on can exercise their specialist skills towards the common goal of financial excellence in their organisations.

DATA THAT MAKES SENSE

Managers, indeed, all of us, are deluged with business data. It comes from internal operating reports, the daily press, business magazines and many other sources. Much of this data is incomprehensible. We know the meaning of the words used separately, but, used collectively, they can be mystifying. Figure 1.1 illustrates the problem. The individual words 'shares', 'profits' and 'cash flow' are familiar to us, but we are not sure how they fit together to determine the viability of the business and articles written about the subject are not much help – they seem to come up with a new concept each month.

Is it possible to make the separate pieces shown in (a) into a coherent, comprehensive picture, as shown in (b)? The answer, for the most part, is 'yes'. The big issues in business are:

- assets
- profits
- growth
- cash flow.

These four variables have interconnecting links. There is a balance that can be maintained between them and, from this balance, will come *corporate value*. It is corporate value that is the reason for most business activity and, for this reason, this book focuses on the business ratios that determine corporate value.

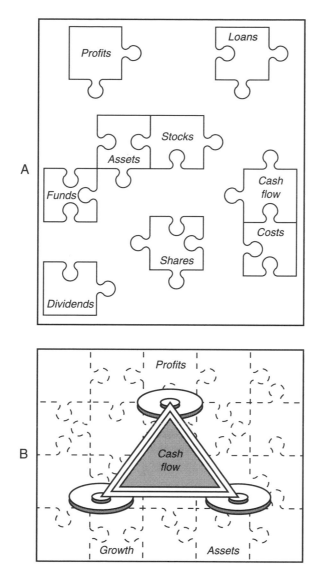

Figure 1.1 Fitting data together for decision making

2 FINANCIAL STATEMENTS

INTRODUCTION

To have a coherent view of how a business performs, it is necessary, first, to have an understanding of its component parts. This job is not as formidable as it appears at first sight, because:

- much of the subject is already known to managers, who will have come in contact with many aspects of it in their work;
- while there are, in all, hundreds of components, there are a relatively small number of *vital* ones;
- even though the subject is complicated, it is based on common sense and can, therefore, be reasoned out once the ground rules have been established.

This last factor is often obscured by the language used. A lot of jargon is spoken and, while jargon has the advantage of providing a useful shorthand way of expressing ideas, it also has the effect of building an impenetrable wall around the subject that excludes or puts off the non-specialist. I will leave it to the reader decide for which purpose financial jargon is usually used, but one of the main aims here will be to show the common sense and logic that underlies the apparent complexity.

Fundamental to this level of understanding of the subject is the recognition that, in finance, there are three – and only three – documents from which we obtain the raw data for our analysis. These are :

- the balance sheet
- the profit and loss account
- the cash flow statement.

A description of each of these, together with their underlying logic, follows.

The balance sheet (B/S)

The balance sheet can be looked on as an engine that has a certain mass/weight from which power is generated in the form of profit. You will probably remember from school the power/weight concept. It is a useful analogy here with which to explain that profit of a known amount must be generated from a balance sheet of a given mass of assets. When we produce a balance sheet for a company, we take a 'snapshot' of the assets used by the company and also of the funds that are related to those assets: however, it is a static document relating to one instant in time. We must, therefore, take repeated 'snapshots' at fixed intervals – months, quarters, years – to see how the assets and funds change with the passage of time.

The profit and loss (P/L) account

The profit and loss account measures the gains or losses from normal operations (and maybe other activities) over a period of time. It measures total income and deducts total cost and both income and cost are calculated according to accounting rules. The majority of these rules are obvious and indisputable, but a small number are not so obvious. Even though founded on solid theory, they can sometimes, in practice, produce results that appear ridiculous. While they have always been subject to review, recent events have precipitated a much closer examination of them. Even while this book is being written, major changes are under way in the definition of cash flow, subsidiary companies and so on.

Cash flow (C/F) statement

The statement of cash flow is a very powerful document. Cash flows into the company when cheques are received and it flows out when cheques are issued, but an understanding of what factors *cause* the flows is fundamental.

Summary

These three statements are not independent of each other, but are linked in the system, as shown in Figure 2.1. Together they give a full picture of the financial affairs of a business. Now let us look at each of these in greater detail.

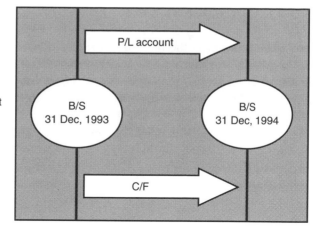

The complete set of accounts consists of:

- opening/closing balance sheets
- profit and loss account
- cash flow statement

Balance sheet

The balance sheet gives a snapshot of the company assets at an instant in time, for example 12 o'clock midnight on 31 December 1993.
Further snapshots will be taken at fixed intervals and, after each interval, movements will have occurred.
The analysis of these movements gives information about the company.

Profit and loss account

This quantifies and explains the gains or losses of the company over the period of time bounded by the two balance sheets.
It derives some values from both balance sheets, so it is not independent of them.
It is not possible to alter a value in the profit and loss account without a corresponding adjustment to the balance sheet. In this way, they support one another.

Cash flow statement

The statement depends on the two balance sheets and the profit and loss account together.
It picks up movements in both, so that, even though this statement is the most recent in time it is now regarded in some quarters as the most important for explaining the financial activities of the company.

Figure 2.1 Elements of accounts are linked together

THE BALANCE SHEET

The balance sheet is the basic document. Traditionally it was always laid out as shown in Figure 2.2. It was a document of two columns that were headed, respectively, 'Liabilities' and 'Assets' and the amounts in these columns added up to the same total. (Note that the word 'Funds' was often used together with or in place of 'Liabilities'.)

The style now used is a single-column layout. The new layout has some advantages, but it does not help the newcomer to understand the logic or structure of the document. For this reason, the two-column layout is mainly used in this publication.

Assets and liabilities

The 'Assets' column contains, simply, a list of items of value owned by the business.

The 'Liabilities' column lists amounts due to parties external to the company. The company is a legal entity separate from its owners, therefore, the term *liability* can be used in respect of amounts due from the company to its owners.

Assets are mainly shown in the accounts at their cost (or unexpired cost). Therefore the 'Assets' column is a list of items of value owned at their cost to the company. It can be looked on as a list of items on which money has been spent.

The 'Liabilities' column simply lists the various sources of that same sum of money. All cash brought into the business is a *source* of funds, while all cash paid out is a *use* of funds. A balance sheet can, therefore, be looked on from this angle – as a statement of sources and uses of funds (*see* Figure 2.3). You will find it very helpful to bear this view of the balance sheet in mind as the theme is further developed (see Chapter 11 for hidden items that qualify this statement to some extent).

Liabilities/Funds	Assets		Balance sheet
Amounts owed by the business	**Things** owned by the business		Traditional form of balance sheet in two columns. This form has now been superseded, but is used here for illustrative purposes.
£1000	£1000		

Figure 2.2 The balance sheet – traditional layout

Balance sheet		Liabilities/Funds	Assets
A most useful way of looking at the financial affairs of a business is to consider its liabilities as *sources* and assets as *uses* of funds.

The two sides are merely two different aspects of the same sum of money, – where it came from and where it went to. | | **Sources** (where money obtained) | **Uses** (where money spent) |
| | | £1000 | £1000 |

Figure 2.3 The balance sheet – sources and uses of funds approach

Balance sheet structure

Figure 2.4 shows the balance sheet divided into five major blocks. These five subsections can accommodate practically all the items that make up the balance sheet. Two of these blocks are on the assets side and three go to make up the liabilities side.

Let us look first at the two blocks of assets, respectively called:

- fixed assets (FA)
- current assets (CA)

These can be considered as 'long' and 'short' types of assets and we will see that this distinction is important here in the case of assets, but even more so in the case of funds.

Current assets (CA)
This box contains all the short-term assets in the company. They will normally convert back into cash within a short time. All the items that find their home in this box can be gathered together under four headings:

- inventories (stocks)
- accounts receivable (trade debtors)
- cash
- miscellaneous.

These items (*see* Figure 2.5) are in constant movement. *Inventories* of raw materials are converted into finished foods. When these are sold they convert into *accounts receivable*. In time, these are converted into *cash* to the company. The *miscellaneous* heading covers any short-term assets not included elsewhere and this part of the balance sheet is usually insignificant. The amount of cash held is often small also, because it is not the function of a company to hold cash. Indeed, where there are large cash balances, there is usually a very specific reason for this, such as a planned acquisition.

The two significant assets in this part of the balance sheet are, therefore, the inventories and accounts receivable – often making up 50 per cent of the total assets of the company.

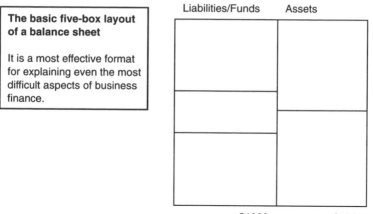

The basic five-box layout
of a balance sheet

It is a most effective format
for explaining even the most
difficult aspects of business
finance.

Figure 2.4 The balance sheet – basic five-box layout

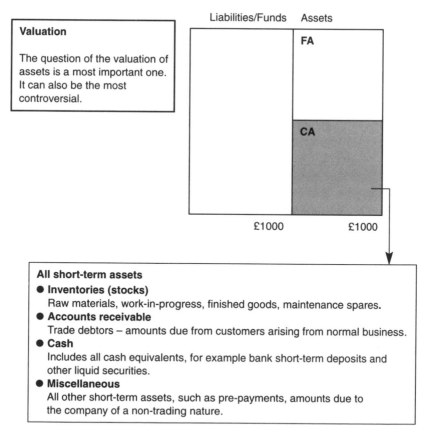

Valuation

The question of the valuation of
assets is a most important one.
It can also be the most
controversial.

All short-term assets
- **Inventories (stocks)**
  Raw materials, work-in-progress, finished goods, maintenance spares.
- **Accounts receivable**
  Trade debtors – amounts due from customers arising from normal business.
- **Cash**
  Includes all cash equivalents, for example bank short-term deposits and
  other liquid securities.
- **Miscellaneous**
  All other short-term assets, such as pre-payments, amounts due to
  the company of a non-trading nature.

Figure 2.5 The balance sheet – the current assets box

Fixed assets

The second major block of assets is that section of the balance sheet that we will refer to as fixed assets (*see* Figure 2.6). We use this term even though the block contains items that do not strictly fall under this heading. A more accurate term would be 'long investment', but the term fixed assets is more convenient.

The items that fall into this block are grouped under three headings:

1 Intangibles

Included under the heading intangibles are all assets that do not have a physical presence. The main one is goodwill. It is an item that gives rise to some controversy and is dealt with further in Appendix 1.

2 Net fixed assets

The large, expensive, long-lasting, physical items used in the operations of the business are included here under the heading *net fixed assets*. They nearly always include land, buildings, machinery and office equipment. The standard value used for each item is original cost less depreciation. In the case of property, adjustments may be made to reflect current values (*see* below).

3 Investments

'*Long-term investments*' are usually long-term holdings of shares in other companies for trading purposes. In group accounts, those companies over which the parent has dominant influence – either by virtue of shareholding or other means – are *totally consolidated*. This means that the separate assets and liabilities are shown in the main balance sheet. The holdings in other associated companies are shown simply as investments.

The question as to whether the balance sheet values should be adjusted to reflect current market values has, for years, been a contentious question. In times of high inflation, property values get out of line – often considerably so – and it is recommended that they be revalued. However, it is important to note that the balance sheet does not attempt to reflect the market value of the separate assets of the total company. Prospective buyers or sellers should, of course, examine these matters closely.

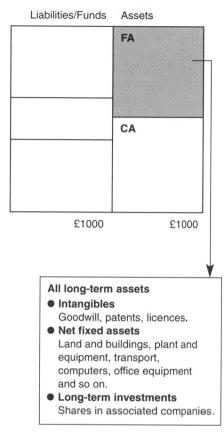

<table>
<tr><td>Liabilities/Funds</td><td>Assets</td></tr>
</table>

Liabilities/Funds   Assets

FA

CA

£1000   £1000

All long-term assets
- **Intangibles**
  Goodwill, patents, licences.
- **Net fixed assets**
  Land and buildings, plant and equipment, transport, computers, office equipment and so on.
- **Long-term investments**
  Shares in associated companies.

Valuation

The question of the valuation of both fixed and current assets is a most important one.
It can also be the most controversial. The accounting rules are detailed and thorough. They rely heavily on cost, but will permit other forms of valuation. However, it must be repeated that the balance sheet does not pretend to reflect the market value of the company *or* the individual assets.

Figure 2.6 The balance sheet – the fixed assets box

Balance sheet structure – liabilities

Figure 2.7 shows three subdivisions of the liabilities column:

- ordinary funds (OF)
- long-term loans (LTL)
- current liabilities (CL)

(At this stage we shall ignore certain types of funds that do not fit comfortably into the classes equity and loans. Usually the amounts are insignificant, they are dealt with in Appendix 1).

Current liabilities (CL)
Regarding current liabilities (*see* Figure 2.7), the parallel between entries under this and the current assets headings is quite strong. We will return to this relationship again and again.

Long-term loans (LTL)
Long-term loans are mortgages, debentures, term loans, bonds and so on that run for more than a year, and usually for a considerable number of years.

Ordinary funds (OF)
This (*see also* Chapter 12) is the most exciting section of the balance sheet. It is the area where fortunes are made and lost. It is where the entrepreneurs can exercise their greatest skills and where takeover battles are fought to the finish. Likewise it is the place where 'financial engineers' regularly come up with new schemes designed to bring ever-increasing returns to the brave. Unfortunately, it is also the area where most confusing entries appear in the balance sheet.

The most important thing to remember is that the total in the box is the figure that matters, not the breakdown between the categories. Also, while our discussion here centres on publicly quoted companies, everything said applies equally strongly to non-quoted companies. The rules of the game are the same for both.

Note the three major subdivisions illustrated further in Figure 2.8:

- issued ordinary shares
- capital reserves
- revenue reserves.

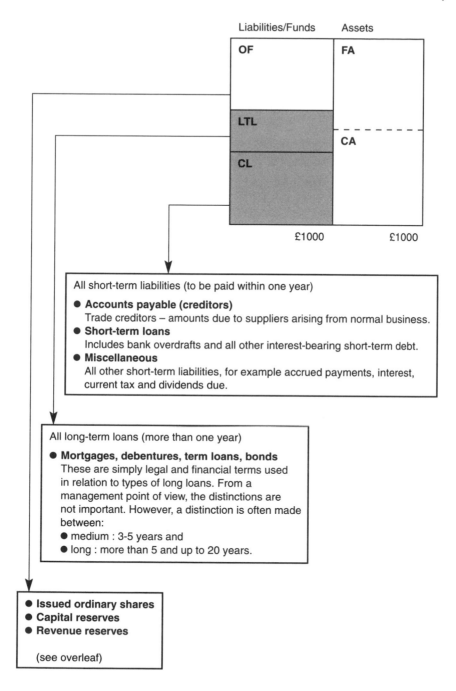

Figure 2.7 The balance sheet – the three subdivisions of the liabilities column

1 Issued ordinary shares

Three different values that are associated with *issued ordinary shares* which will be covered in Chapter 12. These are:

- nominal value
- book value
- market value.

2 Capital reserves

The heading *capital reserves* is used to cover all surpluses accruing to the ordinary shareholder that have not arisen from trading. The main sources of such funds are :

- revaluation of fixed assets
- premiums on shares issued at a price in excess of nominal value
- currency gains on balance sheet items, some non-trading profits, etc.

A significant feature of these reserves is that they cannot be paid out as dividends. In many countries there also are statutory reserves where companies are obliged by law to set aside a certain portion of trading profit for specified purposes – generally to do with the health of the firm. These can be treated as capital reserves.

3 Revenue reserves

These are amounts retained in the company that have come from normal trading profit. Many different terms, names, descriptions are attached to them:

- revenue reserves
- general reserve
- retained earnings etc.

This breakdown, though, is unimportant and the terms used are also unimportant. All the above items belong to the ordinary shareholders. They have all come from the same source and they can be distributed as dividends to the shareholders at the will of the directors.

Summary

We use the five-box balance sheet for its clarity and simplicity. It will be seen later how powerful a tool it is for cutting through the complexities of corporate finance and explaining what business ratios really mean.

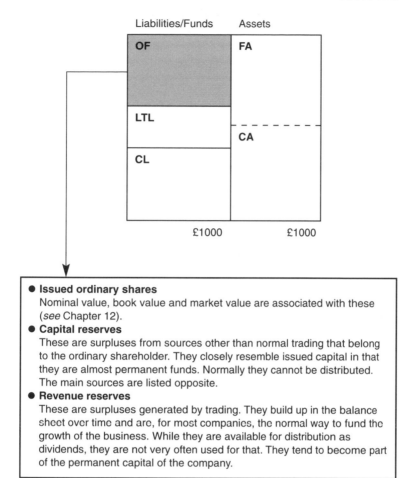

Figure 2.8 The balance sheet – ordinary funds in more detail

3 BALANCE SHEET TERMS

INTRODUCTION

In order to understand and use business ratios we must be clear about *what* it is that is being measured. Definitions and terms used must be precise and robust. We will define four terms each from the balance sheet and the profit and loss account. These are critical values in the accounts that we come across all the time. In any discussion of company affairs, these terms turn up again and again, under many different guises and often with different names. The five-box balance sheet layout will assist us greatly in this section.

THE TERMS USED

The four terms used in the balance sheet are very simple but important:

- total assets
- capital employed
- net worth
- working capital.

Total assets (TA)

You will see from Figure 3.1 that the definition is straightforward :

FA   +   CA   =   TA

£600   +   £400   =   £1000

However, very often we use the term total assets when we are really more interested in the left-hand side of the balance sheet where the definition more properly is:

OF   +   LTL   +   CL   =   TA

£450   +   £250   +   £300   =   £1000

We must be able to see in our mind's eye the relationship that exists between total assets and other balance sheet definitions.

Sometimes we come across the term, *total tangible assets* (the matter of intangibles is discussed further in Appendix 1).

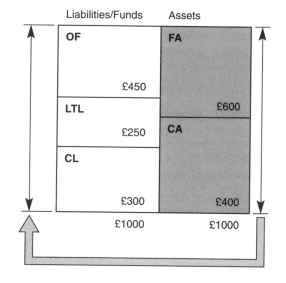

Total assets (TA)

| Liabilities/Funds | Assets |

OF	FA
£450	£600
LTL	
£250	CA
CL	
£300	£400
£1000	£1000

Total assets

The value of total assets of £1000 can be arrived at in two ways:

1 FA + CA   = £600 + £400   = £1000
2 OF + LTL + CL = £450 + £250 + £300 = £1000

Total assets is a value we will use often. As can be seen, it is simply the sum of everything in the balance sheet from top to bottom. This is the same number whether we use the right-hand or left-hand side.

Sometimes it will make more sense to look at this value from the point of view of the assets, and sometimes from the point of view of the funds.
We may use the same expression – total assets – in both situations.

Figure 3.1 Defining total assets

Capital employed (CE)

This is the second important balance sheet term and it is one that is used very widely. Most books on finance give the definition of capital employed as being:

FA + investments + inventory, accounts receivable, cash – accounts payable and short-term loans

To disentangle this definition, look at Figure 3.2 and you will see that it means:

FA + CA – CL = CE

£600 + £400 – £300 = £700

From this same figure, we can see that it also comprises the two upper left-hand boxes of the balance sheet, which gives the definition:

OF + LTL = CE

£450 + £250 = £700

These definitions are identical.

In the first case, we start off at the top right-hand side, work down through fixed assets and current assets to the very bottom and then come back up through current liabilities to end up at the long-term loans line.

In the second case, we start at the top left-hand side and work our way down through ordinary funds and long-term loans.

Either way, we can see that the distinction between total assets and capital employed is that all the *short-term liabilities* in the current liabilities box are omitted from capital employed. Capital employed, therefore, includes only the *long-term funds* sections of the balance sheet.

Many analysts place great emphasis on this section of the balance sheet. They say, with justification, that it represents the long-term foundation funds of the company. In looking at company performance they are concerned to ensure that profits are sufficient to keep this foundation intact. However, others will argue that in the current liabilities category we have, normally, bank borrowings that are, in theory, very short term but are, in reality, permanent funds. They should therefore be included in the funding base when calculating rates of return.

Capital employed (CE)

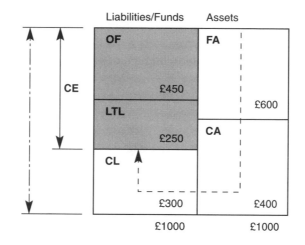

Capital employed

Capital employed can be arrived at in two ways:

FA + CA − CL = £600 + £400 − £300 = £700
OF + LTL   = £450 + £250   = £700

Capital employed is a widely used term. It defines the long-term funds in the balance sheet. We will often see a rate of return expressed as a percentage of this value.

The common definition is total assets less current liabilities. We can see that this is equivalent to owner's funds plus long loans (see Appendix 1 for special items).

Figure 3.2 Defining capital employed

Net worth

This third term brings us to the top left-hand box only of the balance sheet. We have already looked at this box in some detail (*see* Chapter 2), but it emerges here again with a new name – net worth. We know from the previous pages that the following values are included here:

- issued ordinary shares
- capital reserves
- revenue reserves.

Accordingly, the first definition of net worth is the sum of the above three items, amounting to £450.

For the second definition we can use the same method that we used for capital employed. That is, we work our way down through the assets and back up through the liabilities to arrive at the same value of £450:

$$FA \quad + \quad CA \quad - \quad CL \quad - \quad LTL \quad = \quad NW$$

$$£600 \quad + \quad £400 \quad - \quad £300 \quad - \quad £250 \quad = \quad £450$$

The term net worth emphasises this latter definition. It says to us that the real value in this box is determined by the value of all the assets less all external liabilities, both short and long. This is simple common sense. The shareholders, stake in the company is simply the sum of the assets less outstanding loans.

The first way of looking at this box is by means of the accounting definition, where shares are issued and reserves are accumulated over time using all sorts of accounting rules and conventions. The latter is a more pragmatic approach: simply take all the values on the assets side of the balance sheet and deduct outstanding loans – anything left is shareholders' money, no matter what name we give it. However, if *book* values for assets are close to *actual,* both approaches give almost the same answer.

The amount of realism in the net worth figure, then, depends entirely on the validity of the asset values.

Net worth (NW)

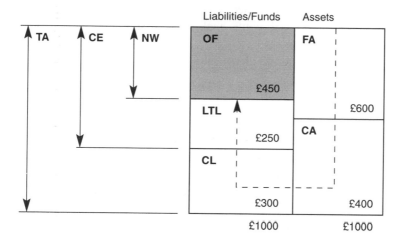

Net worth

The value of NW can be arrived at in two ways:

TA – CL – LTL   = £1000 – £300 – £250 = £450
OF (issued + capital reserves + revenue reserves) = £450

Net worth is another term often used to refer to the top
left-hand box in the balance sheet.
Because it is such a significant section, more than one
name is attached to it.
Net worth has the advantage that it expresses the reality
that the value in this section is derived from:
the total assets less the total external liabilities.

Figure 3.3 Defining net worth

Working capital (WC)

This fourth and final balance sheet term is illustrated in Figure 3.4. It is an important term that we will come back to again and again in our business ratios.

The widely used definition of working capital is :

$$CA \quad - \quad CL \quad = \quad WC$$

$$£400 \quad - \quad £300 \quad = \quad £100$$

This figure is a measure of liquidity. We can consider liquidity as an indicator of cash availability. It is clearly not the same thing as wealth: many people and companies who are very *wealthy* do not have a high degree of *liquidity*. This happens if the wealth is tied up in assets that cannot be converted into cash easily. For instance, large farm and plantation owners have lots of assets, but may have difficulty in meeting day-to-day cash demands – they are very rich but illiquid. So, it is true for companies too that it is not sufficient to have assets; it is necessary to ensure that these are sufficiently liquid to meet ongoing cash needs.

We have an alternative definition in Figure 3.5, that looks at working capital from the *left-hand side* of the balance sheet. This definition is perhaps more relevant to real situations. Here, we see that it can be calculated as:

$$OF \quad + \quad LTL \quad - \quad FA \quad = \quad WC$$

$$£450 \quad + \quad £250 \quad - \quad £600 \quad = \quad £100$$

This definition is not often used but it is a very important way of looking at the structure of a company.

The working capital is determined by the long-term funds that are not tied up in long-term assets. When a business is being set up, adequate funds of this type must be provided and, when there is a need to top it up, it must be done either from additional long-term funds *or* the disposal of fixed assets.

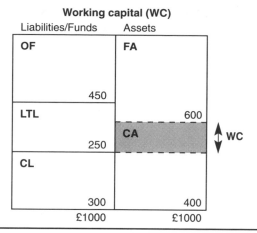

Working capital

The definition of working capital is current assets less current liabilities. A most important value, it represents the amount of day-to-day operating liquidity available to a business.

Operating liquidity is a term used to describe cash and near-cash assets available to meet ongoing cash needs.

A company can be very rich in assets, but short of liquidity if these assets cannot readily be converted into cash.

Figure 3.4 Defining working capital

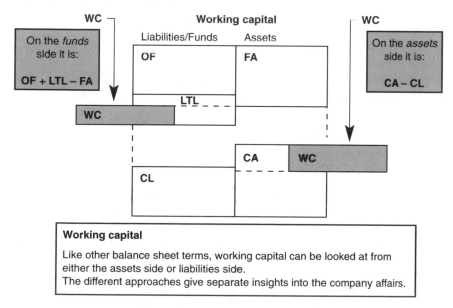

Working capital

Like other balance sheet terms, working capital can be looked at from either the assets side or liabilities side.
The different approaches give separate insights into the company affairs.

Figure 3.5 Alternative definition of working capital

4 PROFIT AND LOSS ACCOUNT

INTRODUCTION

Figure 4.1 identifies where the profit and loss account fits into the set of accounts. It is a link or bridge between the opening and closing balance sheets of an accounting period. Its function is to identify the *total revenue earned* and the *total costs incurred* over that period. The difference between these two values is the *operating profit*. It is, therefore, a document that relates to a very precise time period. There are many accounting rules to do with the identification of revenue and costs.

Total revenue earned

Total revenue earned is generally the amount invoiced and, in most situations, there is no problem with its accurate identification. However, there could be more than one view on the subject of what constitutes total revenue in the second year of, say, a large, three-year civil works project. Also, if we are an engineering company and we sell a warehouse, is that part of revenue?

Total costs incurred

The figure for *total costs* can give rise to more intractable problems. Two rules will help to identify costs that must be included:

- those costs that relate directly to the revenue, for example the direct cost of the goods sold and
- those costs that relate to the time period covered by the accounts, such as staff salaries for the period.

Even with these rules, however, there are still many areas where the decision could go either way. Should research and development costs be charged in the year in which they were incurred? If we replace the factory roof in a period, is that correctly chargeable as a cost? We could question whether a particular depreciation charge is correct. The list can go on.

The statement of accounting policies attached to all published accounts will give some information regarding this aspect and it is wise to examine it before attempting an analysis of the financial statements.

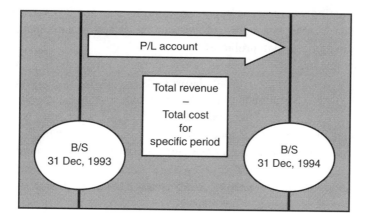

Profit and loss account

The profit and loss account relates very specifically to the time period
31 December 1993 to 31 December 1994.

Total costs are set against total revenue for this period to yield operating
profit.

Relevant costs are:
● those that relate directly to the revenue
● those that relate to the time period.

There are many accounting rules to do with the identification of cost
and revenue. Particularly in the cost area some items can be interpreted
in different ways.

Therefore, in the analysis of a company's accounts it is well to ask what
important assumptions have been made that have had an effect on the
final profit.

Figure 4.1 Place of the profit and loss account in company accounts

In a situation where accountants can sometimes differ, it is not surprising that non-accounting managers go astray. One or two basic signposts will eliminate many common problems.

The profit and loss as such is not concerned with cash flow, which is covered by a separate statement. However, the distinction between *profit* and cash flow is a common cause of confusion. For instance, employees' pay incurred but not paid must be charged as *costs*. On the other hand, payments to suppliers for goods received are *not* costs, simply cash flow. Costs are incurred when goods are consumed, *not* when they are purchased or paid for.

Cash spent on the *purchase of assets* is not a cost, but the corresponding *depreciation* over the following years *is*.

A *loan repayment* is not a cost because an *asset* (cash) and a *liability* (loan) are both reduced by the same amount, so there is no loss in value by this transaction.

In recent years, the question of *extraordinary items* has been much discussed. The issue here is whether large, one-off gains or losses should be included with normal trading activities. We can readily accept the argument that these should be set to one side and not allowed to distort the normal operating results and this was the approach used in producing accounts for many years. However, in some companies, the rule was used selectively. Items *became* extraordinary or otherwise in order to present the desired picture. The rule has been changed to avoid this possibility of distortion.

Finally, the question of *timing* is vital. Having established what the true costs and revenue are, we must locate them in the correct time period. The issue arises just before and just after the cut-off date between accounting periods. As shown in Figure 4.2 we may have to move revenue or costs forwards or backwards to get them into their correct time periods.

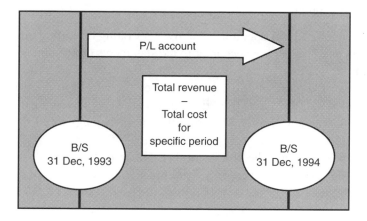

Timing adjustments

Revenue and costs occurring in a period must be adjusted with adjoining periods to ensure that each period is credited and charged *only* with what is appropriate, as shown below.

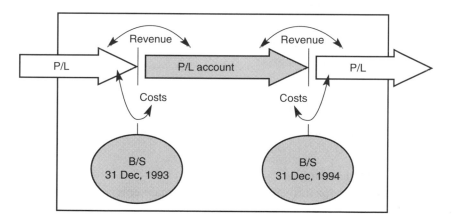

Figure 4.2 The profit and loss account – timing adjustments

Profit/loss – terms

Total revenue less total operating cost gives operating or trading profit. This is the first profit figure we encounter in the statements of account.

From this starting point we identify four basic financial terms that we require from the profit and loss account. They are related to the way profit is distributed. All the assets used in the business have played a part in generating this operating profit. Therefore this profit belongs to all those who have provided the assets.

Figure 4.3 illustrates the process of distribution or 'appropriation' as it is called in the textbooks. There is a fixed order in the queue for distribution as follows:

- to the lenders
- to the taxation authorities
- to the shareholders.

At each of the stages of appropriation the profit remaining is given a precise term. Stripped of the non-essentials the following is a layout of a standard profit and loss appropriation account. When looking at a set of accounts for the first time it may be difficult to see this structure because the form of layout is not as regular as we see in the balance sheet. However if one starts at the profit before tax figure it is usually possible to work up and down to the other items shown:

- **PBIT** – Profit before interest and tax
        Deduct **interest**

- **PBT** – Profit before tax
        Deduct **tax**

- **PAT** – Profit after tax
        Deduct **dividend**

- **RE** – Retained earnings
  (see Appendix 1 for further discussion of unusual items)

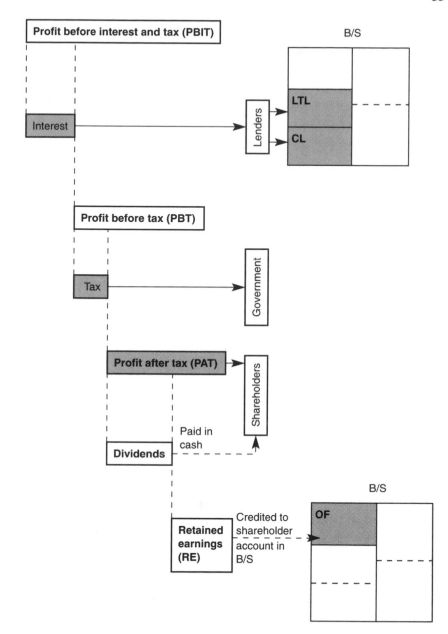

Figure 4.3 The profit and loss account – distribution, or, appropriation

WORKING DATA

Throughout the various stages of the book we will work with two sets of data:

- those the the *Example Co. PLC* have been devised to highlight various aspects of accounts and show the calculation of ratios;
- those of the FT-SE Companies 1990 are an aggregated (selected) set of accounts made up from the separate accounts of 58 companies included in the FT-SE 100 Share Index (*see* Appendix 2 for details). This data is used to derive the standards and norms we need for the different ratios used in our analysis.

Figure 4.4 on the opposite page shows for the example company plc:

- the balance sheet
- the profit/loss account
- share data.

It is worth while spending a moment looking over the now familiar five-box balance sheet and the structured profit/loss account to become familiar with the figures. They will be used a lot in the following chapters.

Please review the following items:

fixed assets
current assets

current liabilities
long-term loans
ordinary funds

PBIT
  Interest
PBT
  Tax
PAT
  Dividend
RE

Example Co. plc

Balance sheet

Liabilities/Funds			Assets		(£000 000s)
Ordinary funds	£	£	**Fixed assets**	£	£
Issued ordinary shares	80		Intangibles	0	
Capital reserves	60		Net fixed assets	440	
Revenue reserves	220		Long-term investments	40	
		360			
Long-term loans					
					480
		200			
			Current assets		
Current liabilities			Inventories	128	
Accounts payable	140		Accounts receivable	160	
Short-term loans	60		Cash	20	
Miscellaneous	40		Miscellaneous	12	
		240			320
		800			800

Profit and loss account

		£	£
Sales			1120
Operating costs			1008
PBIT			112
	Interest	20	
PBT			92
	Tax	32	
PAT			60
	Dividends	24	
RE			36

Share data

Number of ordinary shares	= 320 000 000
Market price of share	= £2.25

Figure 4.4 Working data – the Example Co. PLC

FT-SE SUMMARY

The *Financial Times*-Stock Exchange (FT-SE) 100 Share Index is the most widely quoted barometer of equity performance in the UK. The share price of 100 of the largest quoted companies are its constituents. These companies are the flagships of UK industry. A selection of these companies has been taken to provide aggregate data for the calculation of ratios that can be used as standards or norms for good industrial performance.

All UK quoted companies are grouped into more than 30 industrial sectors. It was largely on the basis of their sectors that the selection was made. Businesses from the financial sectors, mining, property and so on were considered to be rather specialised to include in a general average. Some other companies were not included because it was too difficult to obtain comparable figures for a five-year period (*see* Appendix 2 for a list of all the companies included in the sample).

From seventeen industrial sectors that are represented in the sample, six have been chosen to illustrate the variations in performance that arise from the nature of the business. The ones selected are those that are fairly representative and which provide useful contrasts over a number of business ratios. The sectors are:

- food retailing
- food manufacturing
- chemicals
- stores
- brewers and distillers
- health and household.

Aggregated accounts for selected FT-SE companies 1990

Balance sheet

Liabilities/Funds			Assets	(£000 000 000s)	
Ordinary funds	£	£		£	£
Issued ordinary shares	19.2		**Fixed assets**		
Capital reserves	8.8		Intangibles	5.5	
Revenue reserves	62.7		Net fixed assets	96.0	
		90.7	Long-term investments	14.0	
Long-term loans					
					115.5
		42.0	**Current assets**		
Current liabilities			Inventories	28.8	
Accounts payable	33.9		Accounts receivable	31.6	
Short torm loans	11.9		Cash	19.2	
Miscellaneous	17.2		Miscellaneous	0.6	
		63.0			80.2
		195.7			195.7

Profit and loss account

	£	£
Sales		205.5
PBIT		27.8
Interest	4.6	
PBT		23.2
Tax	7.0	
PAT		16.2
Dividends	7.3	
RE		8.9

Figure 4.5 Working data – the FT-SE Companies 1990

Part 11

OPERATING PERFORMANCE

5 MEASURES OF PERFORMANCE: INTRODUCTION

USING THE BALANCE SHEET AND PROFIT AND LOSS ACCOUNT TOGETHER

Four important terms have been identified from the profit and loss account. Three of these will be associated with three others we identified earlier from the balance sheet and, from this association, we can start the analysis of company accounts.

To discuss company performance, the lower section of Figure 5.1 shows three of the terms from the profit and loss account (profit before interest and tax [PBIT]; profit before tax [PBT]; profit after tax [PAT]) in parallel with three from the balance sheet (total assets; capital employed; net worth) for the Example Co. PLC. Performance is measured by various relationships between these two sets of values.

However, we have a choice as to which value we use from each statement. Profit before interest and tax could be measured against total assets or capital employed or net worth and, likewise, with profit before tax and profit after tax. This gives us nine possible *measures of performance*. In practice, we sometimes meet with each one of them and even with some other variations.

These linkages between values from the balance sheet and values from the profit and loss account are given different names and these come and go, becoming popular for a while and then disappearing again. A selection of these could be:

- return on assets (ROA)
- return on net assets (RONA)
- return on capital employed (ROCE)
- return on invested capital (ROIC) among others.

The point being emphasised here is that these are not *different* ratios: they are all measuring return on assets and the name used does not matter. What *is* important, however, is that we know *which* profit and loss figure is being related to *which* balance sheet figure.

This book will use two measures only. These two have been carefully selected and are as illustrated in Figure 5.2. This does not imply that these are the only correct ones or that all others are deficient in some way. However, they are two of the better measures. There is sound logic for choosing them over certain other ones.

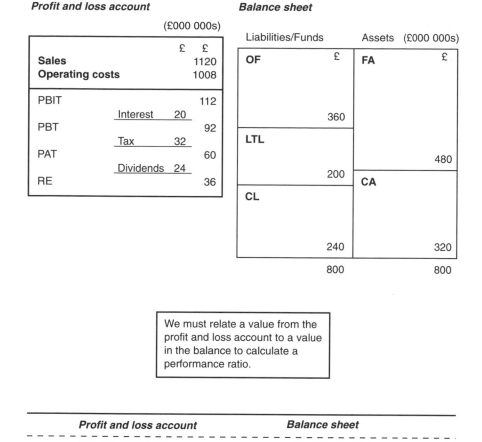

Figure 5.1 Important terms from the profit and loss account using data from the Example Co. PLC

THE RATIOS RETURN ON TOTAL ASSETS AND RETURN ON EQUITY

The two ratios chosen here for the measurement of company performance are illustrated in Figure 5.2. These are:

- *return on total assets* (ROTA) which gives a measure of the operating efficiency of the total business and the method of calculation is profit before interest and tax/total assets and the answer arrived at is 14 per cent in this case.
- *return on equity* (ROE) which assesses the return to the shareholder and this is calculated by putting profit after tax over ordinary funds and the answer is 16.6 per cent in this case.

The significance of these numbers will be examined in Chapter 6. In the opinion of the author these are the two fundamental performance ratios. This said, there are many possible variations to them and some may well be more suitable for particular types of businesses than these. Probably the one next in importance is return on capital employed. As we saw earlier in Chapter 3, capital employed is the figure we get by deducting current liabilities from total assets. The corresponding profit and loss value used is profit before interest and tax with the possible deduction of interest on short-term loans. Because a smaller denominator is used in calculating return on capital employed we would expect a higher answer than for return on total assets.

When new expressions for these ratios are encountered it is often not clear which profit and loss value is being measured against which balance sheet value. Then the question to ask is 'How is it calculated?' When you know what the calculation method is, it is as easy to work with one combination as another. However, there is a certain logic that should be followed, which is that, if the value from the balance sheet includes loans, then the profit and loss value should include the corresponding interest charge and vice versa. This rule is sometimes not adhered to and therefore the resulting answers are fairly meaningless.

Profit and loss account

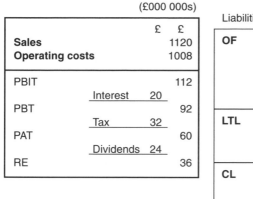

(£000 000s)

	£	£
Sales		1120
Operating costs		1008
PBIT		112
	Interest	20
PBT		92
	Tax	32
PAT		60
	Dividends	24
RE		36

Balance sheet

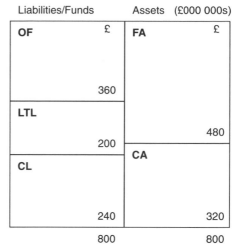

Liabilities/Funds   Assets   (£000 000s)

OF	£	FA	£
	360		
LTL			480
	200	CA	
CL			
	240		320
	800		800

Of all the possible combination of values from the profit and loss account and the balance sheet. Which measures are most appropriate?
The following two are selected.

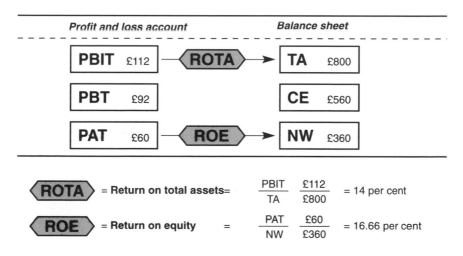

Figure 5.2 The two measures of performance used in this book: return on total assets and return of equity applied to data from the Example Co. PLC

BALANCE SHEET LAYOUTS

A number of alternative forms of layout are used in presenting accounts, particularly for the balance sheet. While the layout itself does not affect any of the numbers, it can be difficult when faced with an unfamiliar format to find where items are located and what the values for total assets, capital employed and so on are.

The first point to remember is that the items within each of the five boxes will always appear grouped together – they are never scattered around among other items. Sometimes, however, the total only of a subsection will appear in the balance sheet proper while the detail is to be found in the 'notes to accounts'.

Given the five-box grouping, it follows that there is only a limited number of ways in which the boxes can be arranged. In Figure 5.3 one such rearrangement is shown. It is easy to see how the items in the two-column format have been reordered into a single vertical column. This type of layout has the advantage that corresponding values for successive years can be laid out side by side. They are then easy to compare. In this format total assets and total funds are also emphasised.

The headings 'Creditors: amounts falling due within one year' and 'Creditors: amounts falling due after more than one year' are widely used to refer to current liabilities and long-term loans respectively. Overleaf a further variation on this vertical balance sheet is shown.

Balance sheet

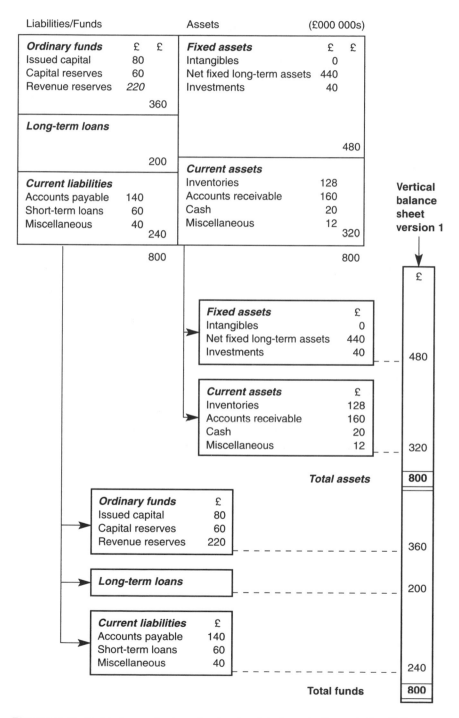

Figure 5.3 Vertical balance sheet version 1 using data from the Example Co. PLC

The second layout in Figure 5.4 is a slightly more sophisticated version, but it is the one most often seen in published accounts. The difference is that the current liabilities figure has been moved out of the liabilities section and is instead shown as a negative value side by side with current assets. The totals of these two sections are netted off to give the figure for working capital.

Both sides of the balance sheet are, accordingly, reduced by the amount of the current liabilities – £240. The original totals amounted to £800, so the new balancing figure is £560. The term often given to this value is total assets less current liabilities. This figure, as mentioned earlier, is capital employed.

The advantage of this layout is that both working capital (current assets less current liabilities) and capital employed values are identified. The disadvantage is that the figure for total assets does not appear anywhere on the balance sheet.

Appendix 1 lists a number of items that we have deliberately omitted from the balance sheet here because we can do most of our analysis without taking them into account. Two of these items are preference shares and minority interests. When they appear in a balance sheet, they will be found at the very bottom of the current layout, as part of the funding of the capital employed.

It is largely a matter of personal preference as to which format is adopted. In the three types of layouts illustrated (the five-box format and vertical versions 1 and 2), practically all possible situations have been covered, so most balance sheets should now make sense. It is a good idea to take whatever form is used and transfer the figures into the familiar five-box format as the significant features will then quickly become evident.

Third and last form of layout

A very popular form of layout is illustrated here.

It is identical to the previous layout, except that current liabilities are deducted from both sides.

A check back to Figure 3.2 will confirm that the final balancing value is what has been defined as capital employed.

Vertical balance sheet version 2

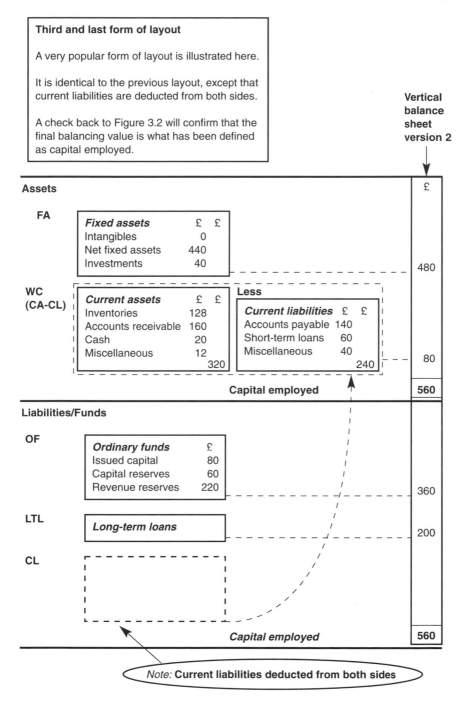

Assets | £

FA

Fixed assets	£	£
Intangibles	0	
Net fixed assets	440	
Investments	40	
		480

WC
(CA-CL)

Current assets	£	£	Less		
Inventories	128		Current liabilities	£	£
Accounts receivable	160		Accounts payable	140	
Cash	20		Short-term loans	60	
Miscellaneous	12		Miscellaneous	40	
		320			240	80

Capital employed | 560

Liabilities/Funds

OF

Ordinary funds	£
Issued capital	80
Capital reserves	60
Revenue reserves	220
	360

LTL

| Long-term loans | 200 |

CL

Capital employed | 560

Note: **Current liabilities deducted from both sides**

Figure 5.4 Vertical balance sheet version 2 using data from the Example Co. PLC

6 OPERATING PERFORMANCE

RETURN ON INVESTMENT (ROI)

The phrase *return on investment* relates to one of the most important concepts in business finance.

The total assets employed in a business create a need for an equivalent quantity of funds to be drawn from the financial markets. These funds have to be paid for at the market rate. Payment can only come from the surplus derived from the efficient use of the assets. It is by relating this surplus to the value of the underlying assets that we find a measure of return on investment.

If this return on investment is equal to or greater than the cost of funds, then the business can be viable. If the rate of return is less, however, the business has no long-term future.

The value of the assets appears in the balance sheet and the corresponding profit is shown in the profit and loss account. Accordingly, we relate the profit and loss account value to the balance sheet value to establish the rate of return. We have already seen the beginnings of this concept in Chapters 4 and 5, but, in this chapter, we examine it more deeply.

The concept of return on investment is universal, but the methods of measurement vary widely. This lack of consistency causes confusion in the minds of many financial and non-financial people alike.

Two measures of return on investment

The two complementary approaches to return on investment that we have already met with will be developed in depth. When these are fully locked into place, variations on the basic themes can be examined and explained without difficulty.

The two measures we will concentrate on are:

- return on total assets (ROTA)
- return on equity (ROE).

These two separate measures are necessary because they throw light on different aspects of the business, both of which are important. Return on total assets looks at the operating efficiency of the total enterprise, while return on equity considers how that operating efficiency is translated into benefit to the owners.

This chapter will concentrate on these two areas. First we will look at methods of calculation, using the Example Co. PLC accounts to explore them. Then we will use the aggregated accounts of the FT-SE Companies 1990 to establish what values can be expected from successful businesses.

RETURN ON EQUITY (ROE)

Figure 6.1 shows how return on equity is calculated. The figure for profit after tax from the profit and loss account is expressed as a percentage of ordinary funds (net worth) in the balance sheet.

This ratio is arguably the most important in business finance. It measures the absolute return delivered to the shareholders in relation to their absolute investment. A good figure brings success to the business – it results in a high share price and makes it easy to attract new funds. These will enable the company to grow, given suitable market conditions, and this in turn leads to greater profits and so on. All this leads to high value and continued growth in the wealth of its owners.

At the level of the individual business, a good return on equity will keep in place the financial framework for a thriving, growing enterprise. At the level of the total economy, return on equity drives industrial investment, growth in gross national product, employment, government tax receipts and so on. It is, therefore, a critical feature of the overall modern market economy as well as to companies within that economy.

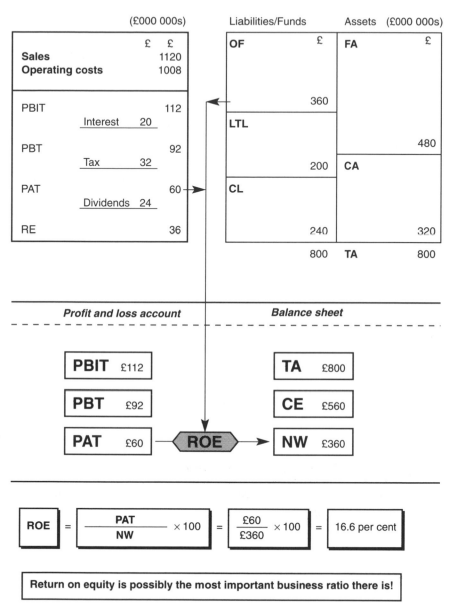

Figure 6.1 Return on equity ratio applied to data from the Example Co. PLC

RETURN ON TOTAL ASSETS (ROTA)

Return on total assets provides the foundation necessary for return on equity. Figure 6.2 shows how this ratio is calculated.

The figure used from the profit and loss account is the total operating profit (profit before interest and tax). This is the amount remaining when total operating cost is deducted from total revenue, but before either interest or tax have been paid. Total operating cost includes direct factory cost, plus administration, selling and distribution overheads.

This operating profit figure is set against the total assets figure in the balance sheet. The percentage relationship between the two values gives the rate of return being earned by the total assets. This ratio is therefore measuring the *efficiency of usage of the total assets.*

Some practitioners contend that the figure taken from the balance sheet should include only the long-term funds and those short-term funds for which a charge is made. The argument is that assets funded by 'free' creditors should not be included in the rate of return calculation. There is considerable merit in this argument, but a counter argument is that the rate of return issue is separate from the funding issue and that assets should produce a return irrespective of the method of funding. For example, some companies choose to fund by suppliers credit, others from a bank loan. The author's view is that, for most companies, the balance of advantage lies with the latter school of thought.

Whichever method of calculation is adopted, return on total assets uses the three main operating variables of the business:

- total revenue
- total cost
- assets employed (some definition of).

It is therefore the most comprehensive measure of total management performance that can be found.

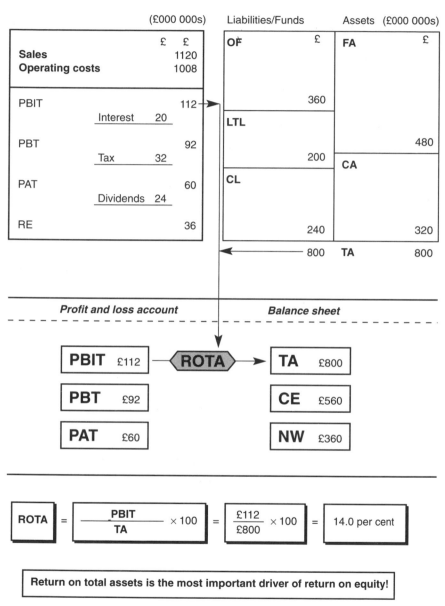

Figure 6.2 Return on total assets ratio applied to data from the Example Co. PLC

STANDARDS OF OPERATING PERFORMANCE

Figure 6.3 shows a summary balance sheet and profit and loss account for the FT-SE Companies 1990.

The ratio values extracted from these accounts are:

- return on total assets – 14.2 per cent
- return on equity – 18 per cent.

We should remember that the return on total assets is pre-tax and return on equity is calculated on the companies' after-tax profit.

These are the rates of return that were achieved by these high-level UK companies in that year. They are obviously all very good performers and are the gold medallists as it were of UK industry.

This is not to say that, because they are the largest, they are the most profitable. Indeed better results are often produced by smaller businesses. However, to reach their pre-eminent position, these companies have consistently produced good results; they have survived and grown over many years.

Their continued success is justification for using an average of their combined results as a good target for other firms to aim for.

The rates of return derived from their combined accounts are very high indeed as it is not so many years since rates of 6 to 8 per cent were considered normal. Of course, the effect of inflation has to be taken into account, but, even allowing for the high levels of inflation experienced in recent years, a return on equity of 18 per cent (after corporation tax) is exceptional. Averages, however, can be deceptive. For this reason the spread of values within the overall group, together with a breakdown over certain sectors, is given in the following pages. (Note: small variations in average values will occur depending on whether calculations are based on the total sample or on the six sectors used from within the sample).

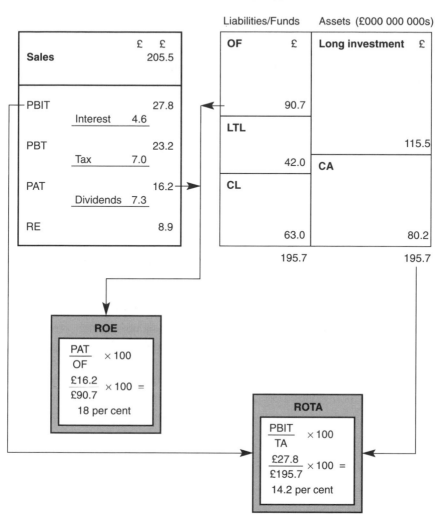

Figure 6.3 Return on total assets and return on equity ratios applied to data from the FT-SE Companies 1990

Return on equity – analysis of FT-SE companies

We have described return on equity as being, probably, the single most important financial ratio we have; it is the great driver of company value. Therefore it is important to know what is happening in the world in terms of this ratio. The following charts throw some light on this.

In Figure 6.4 A, we can see how 50 per cent of all companies in the sample produce return on equity results between 13 per cent and 24 per cent. Only 25 per cent of the sample had results below 13 per cent and, likewise, above 24 per cent.

This lower number can be considered the minimum target to aim for as only 10 per cent of companies fall below a 9 per cent return on equity – it can be looked on as the danger level.

We must remind ourselves that this comparison is being made with first-class companies. Therefore, the overall average figure of 18 per cent would be a first-class performance for a smaller company.

B in Figure 6.4 shows the absolute values for return on equity for the six different sectors and C shows deviations from the average. You can see that the sectors show considerable variation.

Health is by far the best, with an average return on equity of 30 per cent, which is 70 per cent above the average of all companies. At the other end of the scale, brewing has a 13 per cent return on equity, which is 30 per cent below the average.

The two food sectors have very comfortable figures and both chemicals and stores sectors' values are very close to the norm.

As we work our way through the subsidiary ratios, we will see the value drivers that are important in each sector.

All

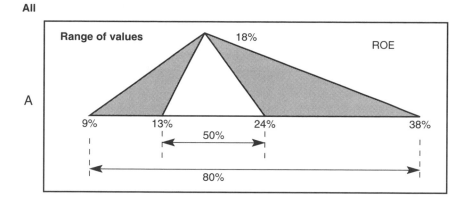

By sectors

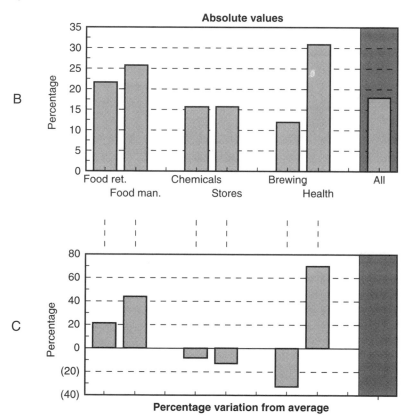

Figure 6.4 Sector values for return on equity for data from FT-SE Companies 1990 using return on total assets ratio

Return on total assets – analysis of FT-SE companies

Return on totals assets is the prime measure of operating efficiency. It has the most important influence on return on equity. Also, it is the ratio over which operations management has most control. The chart will help to set the target for good performance.

In Figure 6.5, A, again we see that the average is 15 per cent and the boundaries for the middle 50 per cent of all companies are 12 and 18 per cent. We can say that a result in *excess* of 18 per cent is excellent and that a result in the region under 12 per cent is only adequate.

The 80 per cent range has a lower boundary of 9 per cent. This number is below an acceptable level of achievement and, except for a temporary situation, is unsatisfactory. Only a very small number of absolutely superb businesses produce results in excess of 20 per cent. Many of these are in the health care business. In the past, some hi-tech companies were in this league.

Sectors

The main feature of the sectoral charts is the lack of variation from the average of most industries. Even though individual companies vary considerably in performance, the sectors, for the most part, conform to the average. Sections B and C in Figure 6.3 display the close correspondence that exists between the results of the first five sectors, which cluster in the 12 and 15 per cent range. The individuality of the sixth sector, health, also stands out clearly.

As we go through the different ratios, we will find that individual sectors are good in some areas of performance and not so good in others. However, health outperforms all other sectors in almost every single ratio and we have already seen how effective this combination is on return on equity values.

All

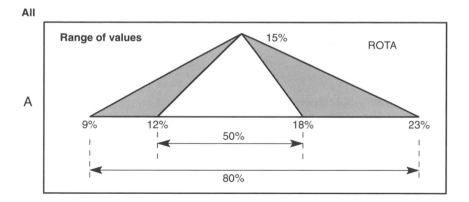

By sectors

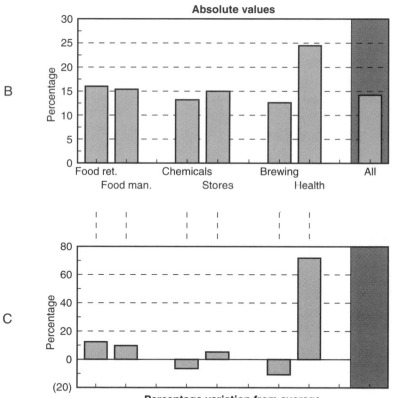

Figure 6.5 Sector analysis of the FT-SE Companies 1990 using return on total assets ratio

The components of return on total assets

Return on total assets is a key tool that can help management enormously in directing its day-to-day activities. However, to be useful, it must first be broken down into its component parts and this will be done in two stages.

The first stage is shown in Figure 6.6. The main ratio is divided into its two main subsidiary ratios:

- margin on sales percentage
- sales to total assets ratio, or, asset turn.

These two values, multiplied, always give the value of return on total assets. Later, each of these ratios will be further broken down to expose greater levels of detail. However, this first split is *so* important that we will take the risk of overemphasising it here. The formula is:

$$\text{Margin} \quad \times \quad \text{Turn} \quad = \quad \text{ROTA}$$

$$\frac{\text{PBIT}}{\text{Sales}} \quad \times \quad \frac{\text{Sales}}{\text{TA}} \quad = \quad \frac{\text{PBIT}}{\text{TA}}$$

$$\frac{£14}{£200} \quad \times \quad \frac{£200}{£100} \quad = \quad \frac{£14}{£100}$$

$$7 \text{ per cent} \quad \times \quad 2 \text{ times} \quad = \quad 14 \text{ per cent}$$

We have now derived two most important ratios. The ratio on the left identifies profit as a percentage of sales and is often described as the *net profit margin*. It is a well-known measure and almost universally used in the monitoring of company profit performance.

The ratio on the right looks at the *total sales achieved by the company in relation to its total assets.* This measure is less often emphasised in the assessment of company performance, but its role in determining the value of return on total assets is just as powerful and important as the profit margin.

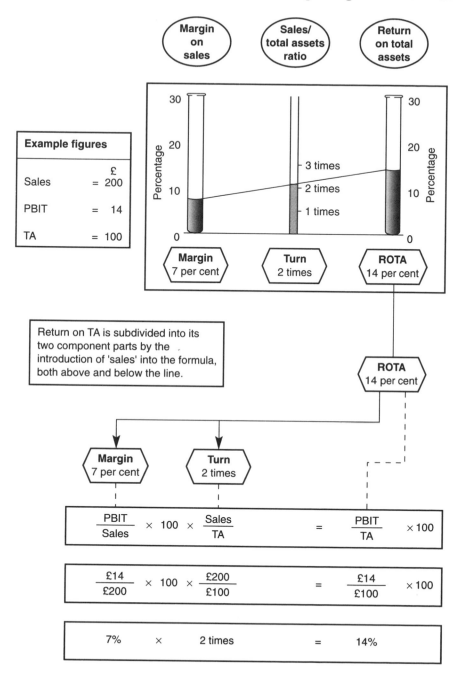

Figure 6.6 The two drivers of the return on total assets ratio

The importance of this concept of the interrelationship of ratios is difficult to exaggerate. To repeat our logic so far:

- return on total assets is the most important driver of return on equity
- return on equity is the most important determinant of company value.

Now we know that the drivers of return on total assets are:

- margin on sales percentage
- sales to total assets ratio.

We have seen that average return on total assets values for companies from many different industrial sectors tend to fall within a fairly narrow band, such as 14 per cent plus or minus 2 per cent. However, the subsidiary ratios that deliver this standardised final result vary widely across different sectors. Figure 6.7 shows some typical values for companies with vastly different profiles.

Example A
Here we see typical figures for a distribution-type company, where low margins in the region of 5 to 7 per cent combine with a high sales to total assets ratio in the region of 2 times.

Example B
Here the opposite applies. Very high margins and low asset turns are typical of companies that require large quantities of fixed assets. The telecommunications sector generates sales margins in the region of 25 per cent. However, their enormous investment in fixed assets means that this margin is only just adequate to make a reasonable return on total assets.

Example C
Here we see fairly average figures, with margins at 10 per cent or less and asset turn values somewhat greater than 1. Quite a number of medium-sized manufacturing companies have this kind of pattern. The difference between success and difficulty in this type of business is often only 2 per cent on margin and 0.1 in the sales to total assets ratio

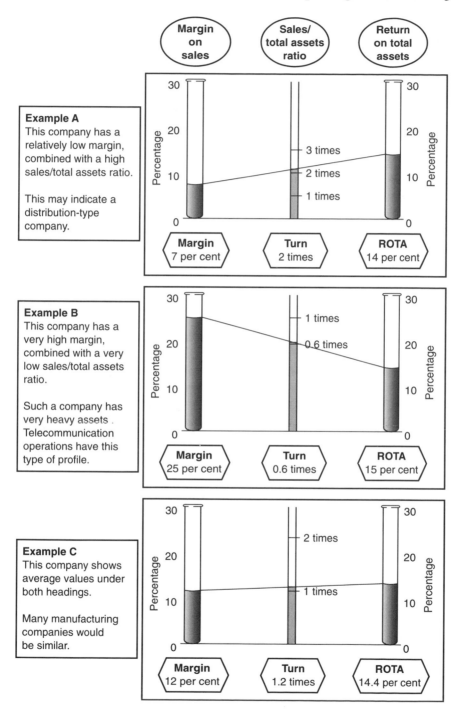

Figure 6.7 Margin on sales and sales to total assets ratios compared to return on total assets ratio values for different types of business

Figure 6.8 illustrates the calculations and results for the FT-SE companies. An average sales margin of 13.5 per cent is delivered 1.1 times to produce a return on total asset value of just over 14 per cent.

For comparison purposes, it is worth remembering that the FT-SE companies have, on average, both large cash holdings and heavy investments in their balance sheets. The effects of these holdings are that assets and profits are increased, but sales are not. Accordingly, we see apparently higher margins and lower sales to total assets ratios than we would expect to see in medium-sized companies.

The range of values charts beneath the figures show that, for the 50 per cent ranges, the margin swings from 9 to 22 per cent, and the asset turn from 0.75 to 1.5 times. Noting the point made above, a rough rule of thumb would be that a margin slightly in excess of 10 per cent, combined with an asset turn of between 1.3 and 1.5 would be where many companies would find a comfortable and reasonably profitable position.

Much of the current emphasis is directed towards achieving a better utilisation of assets. From the Far East we hear stories of fixed assets being used 22 hours out of the 24 and, of course, the Just in Time approach is well known for the dramatic effects it can have on stock levels. Both of these developments will drive up sales to total assets ratios. The *counter-effect*, of course, is that more fierce competition is constantly reducing margins.

It rests with the skill of each management team to discover for itself the unique combination of margin and asset turn that will give their company its own particular, and succesful, market niche.

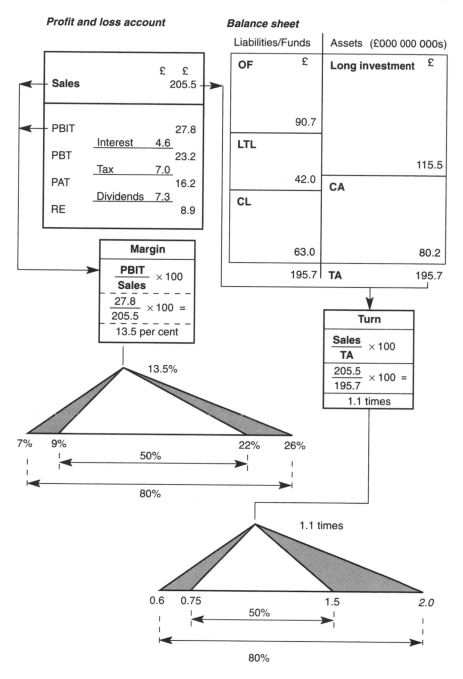

Figure 6.8 Margin on sales and sales to total assets ratio applied to data from FT-SE Companies 1990

Sector parameters – return on total assets

In Figure 6.9, the sector values for margin percentages and asset turn times are illustrated. It is interesting to note that they are almost mirror images of one another. High sales to assets ratios generally reflect low margins and vice versa. The areas where the mirror images do *not* exactly match are where the high and low performers are located.

Sales to Total Assets Ratio

The values shown in Chart A of Figure 6.9 point to a question concerning business performance that is absolutely critical: what level of investment is required to support any given level of sales? The results displayed here help us to understand why some sectors of industry seem to have a built-in advantage over others.

Chart A shows the high sales to total assets ratios inherent in the food industry. While this ratio is high in both sectors – retailing *and* manufacturing – it is more pronounced in the retailing than in the manufacturing area.

Chemicals and stores both have sales to total assets ratios that are approximately 20 per cent above the average, but this advantage is more or less offset by their lower margins – particularly in the case of chemicals. The two sectors are still quite good overall.

When we look to the two final sectors, we see a dramatic contrast. The brewing value is very low, with a sales to total assets ratio of 0.6 times. It may be more informative to turn this ratio upside down and say that it requires £1.60 of assets to carry £1.00 of sales. For any given level of sales, the investment in assets is enormous. In contrast, in the food retailing sector it takes only 45p to support £1.00 of sales. The brewing/distilling sector requires almost four times this investment to produce this result.

In the health sector, we note that the sales to total assets ratio is also below average. However, the two situations are entirely different. The health sector has a margin on sales that compensates by almost 200 per cent for these somewhat high assets whereas the high margins in brewing are still not sufficient to pay the very high investment in this sector.

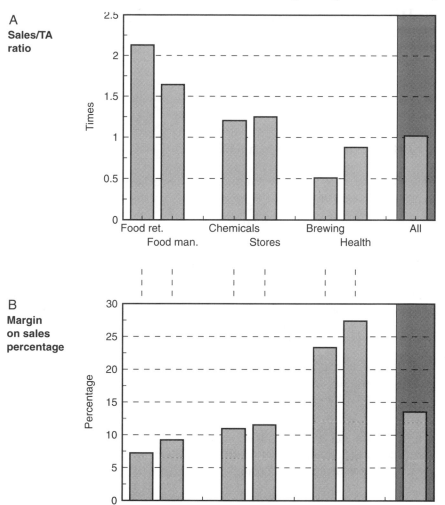

A
Sales/TA ratio

B
Margin on sales percentage

Figure 6.9 Sector values for sales to total assets and margin on sales ratios for data from FT-SE Companies 1990

7 PERFORMANCE DRIVERS

OPERATING PERFORMANCE

The two prime ratios that drive return on total assets have now been identified:

- margin on sales percentage
- sales to total assets ratio

and these are laid out again for the Example Co. PLC in Figure 7.1.

It is on these two drivers that managers must concentrate to improve performance. However, these ratios cannot be operated on directly. Each is dependent on a whole series of detailed results from widely separated parts of the operation which can in turn be expressed in ratio form. What managers need is a system that will enable them to identify and quantify these subsidiary values so that they can:

- set the target value for each ratio that, if achieved, will deliver the required overall performance level
- delegate the achievement of these targets to specific individuals.

The system outlined in the following pages achieves this end. It will be seen that it incorporates all the main elements that appear in both the profit and loss account and balance sheet. Each of the elements is a performance driver and must be managed accordingly.

DRIVERS OF MARGIN ON SALES

At its simplest, we can say that the margin is what is left when the total operating cost is deducted. If the margin were 10 per cent, the total cost would be 90 per cent. The margin can be improved *only* if this 90 per cent can be reduced. To reduce the figure, we must know its component parts. So, the next stage is to identify the separate cost elements and see what percentage each of the main cost elements bears to sales. This operation is illustrated in Figure 7.2.

DRIVERS OF THE SALES TO TOTAL ASSETS RATIO

This ratio is also broken down into its component parts. We identify the main groups of assets straight from the balance sheet and we then express the ratio between each group and the sales figure as shown in Figure 7.3.

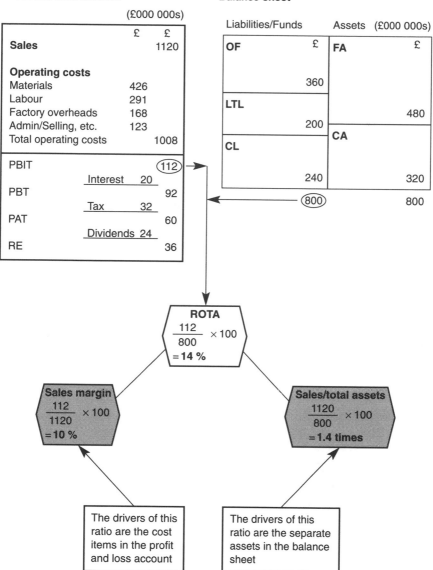

Figure 7.1 Margin on sales and sales to total assets ratios applied to data from the Example Co. PLC

Margin on sales – drivers

Figure 7.2 shows the development of the left-hand side of the model, which is concerned with profit and loss values. The four main cost elements that accumulate to total operating costs are identified as *materials*, *labour*, *factory overheads* and *admin/selling*, *etc*. These large cost groups are used for example purposes; in practice they would be broken down into much more detail.

In the lower part of the diagram, each cost element is shown expressed as a percentage of sales. For instance, the first box shows that materials is 38 per cent (material cost of £426 over sales of £1120 multiplied by 100) . The total of all the various costs is 90 per cent, giving a margin of 10 per cent.

If management wishes to improve this margin, then one or more of the cost percentages must fall. For instance, if the material cost percentage could be reduced by two points, from 38 to 36 per cent, then, other things being equal, the margin percentage would improve by two points to 12 per cent. This margin of 12 per cent would then combine with the sales to total assets ratio of 1.4 times to give an improved return on total assets of 16.8 per cent (that is, 12 per cent multiplied by 1.4).

These cost ratios allow managers to plan, budget, delegate responsibility and monitor the performance of the various functional areas under their control. They can quantify targets for all areas, and calculate the effect of a variation in any one of the subsidiary ratios on the overall performance .

The results achieved by different managers, products and divisions can also be compared and the experiences of the best passed on to the others to help them improve. We must recognise, however, that there are operating factors that the model does not cope with. The variables of selling price, volume and product mix, which have such a powerful impact on profit, are not easily distinguished from other factors in the model. In later chapters these factors will be discussed further.

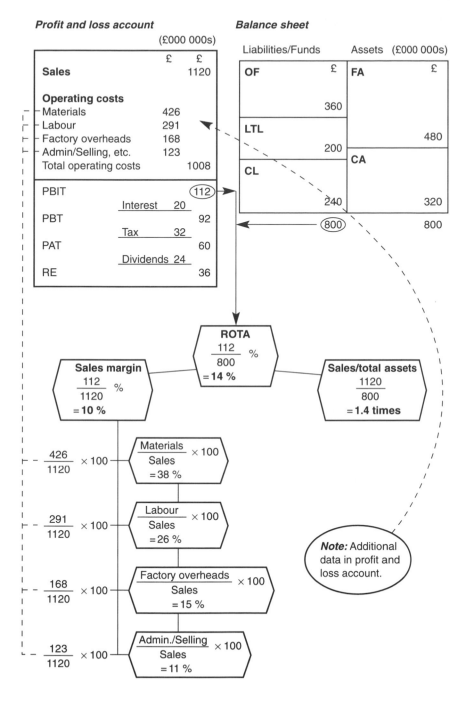

Figure 7.2 Drivers of margin on sales applied to data from the Example Co. PLC

Sales/total assets – drivers

In Figure 7.3 it will be seen that just as the subsidiary values of the left-hand side were derived from the profit and loss account, so these right-hand elements are taken from the balance sheet. Each of the main asset categories is related to sales.

The three major asset blocks in all enterprises are:

- fixed assets
- inventories (stocks)
- accounts receivable (debtors).

The value of each in relation to sales is shown in the subsidiary boxes. For instance, the ratio for fixed assets is 2.5 times (from sales of £1120 divided by fixed assets of £440). Note that the sum of these separate values does not agree with the sales to total assets ratio as did the sales margin on the other side with the operating costs. This is because they are expressed differently. If the reciprocals of the values are taken, the link is clear, as shown at the foot of the diagram.

To managers, this display shows the importance of managing the balance sheet as well as the profit and loss account. For instance, if the total assets could be reduced from £800 to £700, then the sales to total assets ratio would move up from 1.4 to 1.6 times. The effect on the return on total assets would be to increase it from 14 to 16 per cent. If, in addition, the margin were increased by 1 per cent to 11 per cent, then the new return on total assets would be almost 18 per cent (11 per cent × 1.6 times). The original value of 14 per cent is an average value whereas a return on total assets of 18 per cent represents an excellent performance.

In these areas, production managers can work with finance and marketing departments to quantify targets for stock holdings and accounts receivable. The impact of a major capital investment project can also be assessed in profitability terms.

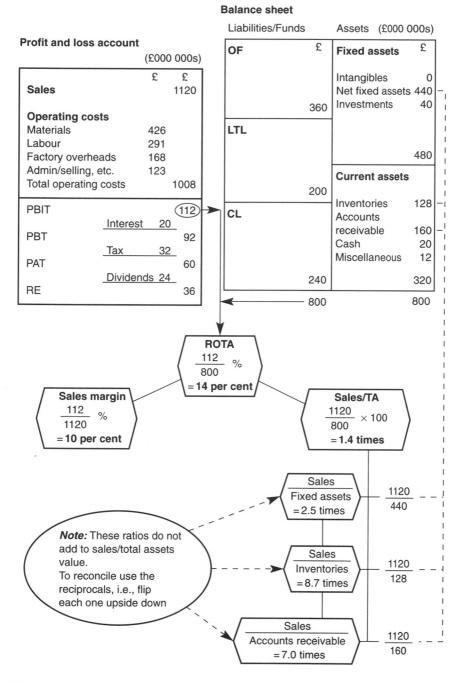

Figure 7.3 Drivers of sales to total assets ratio applied to data from the Example Co. PLC

OPERATING PROFIT MODEL

The complete model is shown in Figure 7.4. It gives a very powerful insight into the parameters of good performance. It enables managers and functions to work better together as a team. It helps with the definition of responsibilities, delegation of authority and target setting. It provides a powerful framework for a management information system. However, there are a number of issues it does not highlight.

First, a business normally deals not just in *one* product, but in a *broad range*. Cost percentages are averages of the cost elements of the individual products. For management control, it is not satisfactory to work with averages because favourable movements in one product will mask adverse movements in another (these issues are dealt with in depth in Chapter 15).

Second, a cost percentage, such as materials, can vary for two totally different reasons:

- a change in the absolute material cost per unit.
- a change in the unit selling price of the product.

The model, however, cannot distinguish between these two causes, despite the fact that one of the most effective ways to reduce the cost percentages is a price increase.

Third, the model does not cope very well with changes in volume, which can be one of the most powerful ways open to a company to improve performance. A volume increase will certainly be picked up by the sales to total assets ratio – a 10 per cent improvement in volume would move this ratio up from 1.4 to 1.54 times – but, because of fixed costs, the volume change is very likely to have an effect on the sales margin too (this subject is also dealt with in Chapter 15).

Fourth, the perceptive reader will have noted that this ratio is dependent on the valuation of the assets in the balance sheet. Difficulties can arise when we compare different businesses or divisions because of the age of plant, different depreciation policies and so on.

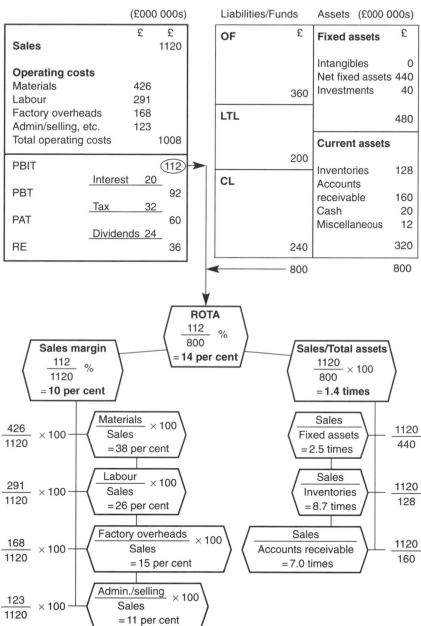

Figure 7.4 Completed operating profit model applied to data from the Example Co. PLC

Model variations

Many business ratios appear under different names or are calculated differently and this can cause some confusion. In the set of ratios we are looking at here, there are two that appear under a number of different guises.

Sales to accounts receivable

This ratio is commonly expressed in terms of day's sales and the method of calculation is shown in Figure 7.5. Instead of the formula we have been using here of sales over accounts receivable, the alternative is to show accounts receivable over sales and multiply the result by 365. The answer represents the average number of days' credit customers take before paying off their accounts.

This ratio is often referred to as *debtor days* or, the *collection period.* The concept of the number of days outstanding is easy to understand. The number is very precise, which means that a slippage of even a few days is instantly identified. Also, figures can be compared with the company's normal terms of trade and the effectiveness or otherwise of the credit control department can, therefore, be monitored.

Companies will vary their methods of calculation to reflect their own business circumstances and to provide answers that make sense to them in particular. For instance:

- VAT may be included in the debtors but not the sales figure and this distortion will have to be removed
- when there is a heavy seasonal variation, the monthly figures calculated in the normal way may not be very helpful and so the company may work, not on an annual sales basis, but on quarterly sales multiplied by four.

Sales to inventories

This calculation is similiar to the one above and is also known as *inventory day.* The inventories link with sales is not so close as that of sales with accounts receivable. It may, therefore, be linked to purchases or usage, whichever gives the most useful guidance.

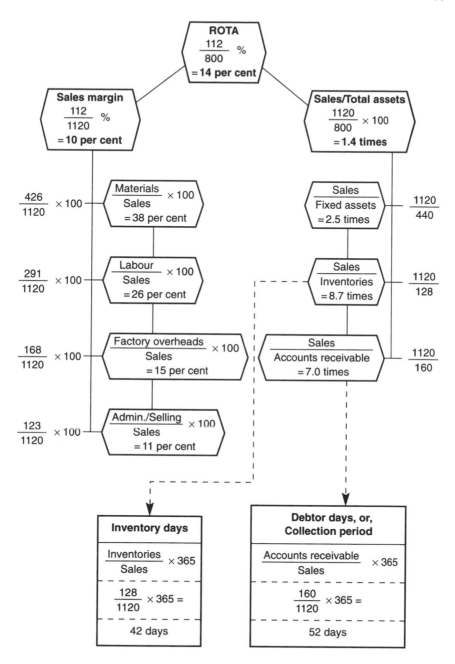

Figure 7.5 Variations to operating profit model applied to data from the Example Co. PLC

Sales to fixed assets ratio and the FT-SE Companies 1990
This ratio, which is one of the strong determinants of company performance, is heavily influenced by the nature of the industry. It is, therefore,
less amenable to management action than are many of the other performance drivers. For many years, it has been difficult for capital-intensive
sectors of industry to earn high returns except where there has been some
element of monopoly.

We can see from Figure 7.6 that the two food sectors are high, while
brewing alone comes out well below the average at 50%.

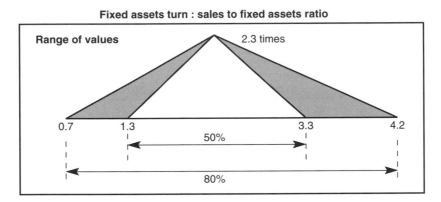

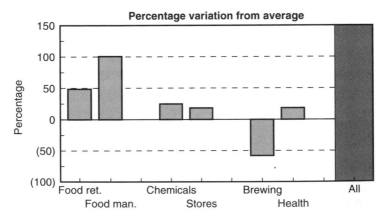

Figure 7.6 Sales to fixed assets ratio and the FT-SE Companies 1990

Inventory days and the FT-SE Companies 1990
An average value of 45 days with lower and upper boundaries for the 50 per cent range of 26 to 67 days emerges in Figure 7.7. The sectoral analysis throws up two major variations – one positive and one negative.

Food retailing has only 18 days. The low inventory requirement is one of the prime contributors to profit in this sector. Brewing, on the other hand, carries almost 80 days of inventory, that is approximately 4 times the level of the first sector. This high inventory, when added to the heavy fixed assets employed, makes it difficult for the sector to achieve a good return on capital.

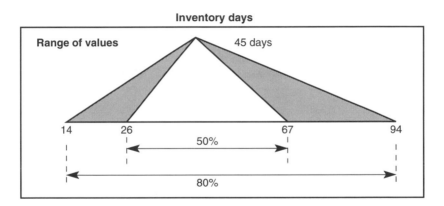

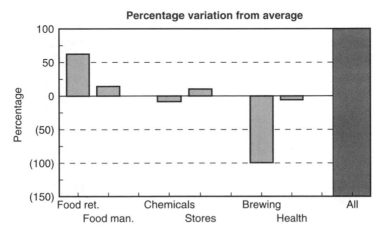

Figure 7.7 Inventory days and the FT-SE Companies 1990

Debtor days and the FT-SE Companies 1990

An average value of 60 days with lower and upper boundaries for the 50 per cent range of 43 to 82 days results from the summary figures shown in Figure 7.8. Accounts receivable are somewhat higher than inventory on average. For this ratio the two extreme sectors are food retailing and health.

Food retailing is very positive with almost no accounts receivable, as we could have guessed from our own shopping experiences. Health has a heavy negative variance with 80 days of credit being given to customers. It is obvious that producers in this area help to fund their distributors and that credit to customers is a marketing tool for them.

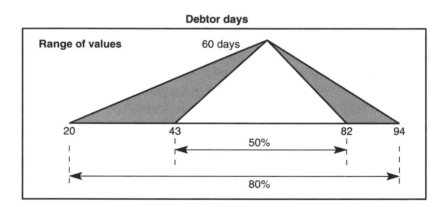

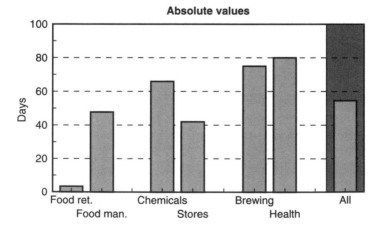

Figure 7.8 Debtor days and the FT-SE Companies 1990

Part III

CORPORATE LIQUIDITY

8 CASH FLOW CYCLE

CORPORATE LIQUIDITY

A company that cannot produce cash to meet its day-to-day requirements has run out of *liquidity* and is in a very serious condition. Ironically, this is so *even if* it is generating good profits currently or has accumulated them in the past. When *cash* runs out, the company's management has lost the power to make independent decisions. An outside agency, such as an unpaid creditor or a bank whose loan is in default, will, effectively, decide the fate of the company instead of its management. That fate could be bankruptcy, a forced reconstruction, an involuntary takeover or the company could be allowed to continue in some altered form. The reality is that management has lost control and it is most likely that the owners, too, have lost their entire investment.

One may well ask *how* can this happen if profits are good. The answer is that it *does* happen and for reasons that will become clearer later. Loss of profits is often the immediate cause of the disaster, but it is not uncommon even when companies are making good profits. Indeed, profitable and rapidly growing small companies often run out of cash. They then pass out of the hands of the original owner or entrepreneur.

This chapter will examine liquidity and the cash flow factors that drive it. It will look at how we can measure a company's liquid health and what the forces are that act to its detriment or benefit.

THE CASH CYCLE

The flow of cash through an organisation is often compared with the flow of blood through the body. When we look at the cash flow diagram in Figure 8.1, the reason for this is obvious. Cash is in continuous circulation through the 'arteries' of the business carrying value to its various 'organs'. If this flow is stopped, or even severely reduced for a time, then serious consequences result. This diagram shows part of the total cash cycle, the part that we refer to as working capital. It represents the operating day-to-day cash flow. Central to the system is a cash tank, into and out of which cash flows constantly. **It is crucial to the independent survival of the business that this tank does not run dry.**

Shown beneath the cash tank is a spare, or, supplementary supply, representing unused short-term loan facilities.

Day-to-day liquidity consists of these two separate cash reservoirs. The main flow of cash into the reservoir comes from accounts receivable (these are the customers who pay for the goods or services sold by the company).

The main cash out-flows can be identified under two main headings:

- payments to accounts payable, that is suppliers of raw materials and other main purchases.
- payments of pay or salaries to the staff and payments of all other operating expenses of the business.

In day-to-day operations, accounts payable supply raw materials. These, in time, pass through work in progress into the finished goods category. During this conversion, other cash is absorbed by them in the form of labour and expenses.

In due course, these goods are sold. Value passes down the artery into the accounts receivable box, from which it flows back into the cash reservoir to complete the cycle.

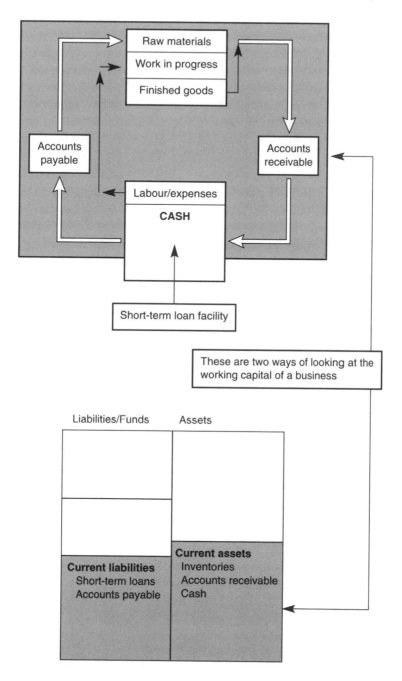

Figure 8.1 The operating cash cycle and working capital

To Figure 8.1, two further inputs are added that cause the cash in circulation to increase :

- profit and loss account
- depreciation.

The profit and loss account input is easy to understand because normally goods are sold at a profit. For instance if goods that are held in stock at a total cost of £100 are sold at a price of £125, the £25 profit will very quickly come into the business in the form of extra cash.

Depreciation is, perhaps, a little more difficult to understand. It is often referred to as a source of funds. Some years ago we would have seen the definition:

operating cash flow = operating profit + depreciation

It is not easy to see why this should be. What is so special about depreciation? The answer is that, for most companies, depreciation is the only cost item in the profit and loss account that does not have a cash out-flow attached to it. While referred to as a source of cash, it is really the *avoidance* of a cash out-flow. This point is more fully developed overleaf.

It must be emphasised that, even though depreciation does not have a related cash out-flow, it is a true cost nevertheless. The relevant cash out-flow has simply taken place at an earlier time. At the time the associated fixed assets was purchased, the cash cost was not charged against profits. It was, instead, charged to the balance sheet. As the asset is used up, an appropriate amount of cost is released into the profit and loss account and this is what depreciation is all about.

Figure 8.2 shows that, at the completion of every full cycle, the amount of cash available to the system is increased by the profit earned plus the depreciation charged.

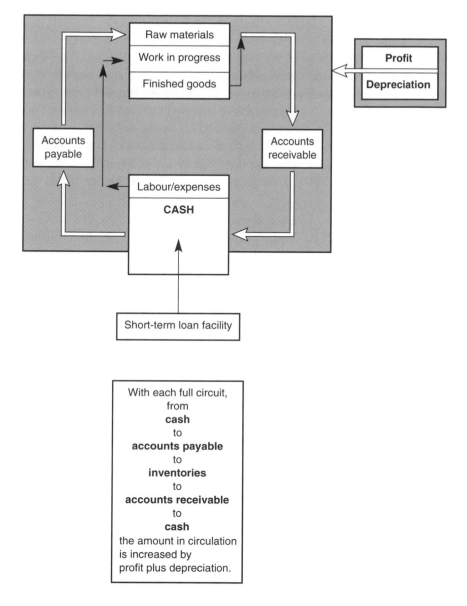

Figure 8.2 The operating cash cycle and the role of profit and depreciation

Depreciation and cash flow

The example in Figure 8.3 illustrates the relationship between depreciation and cash flow that can give rise to much confusion. The example uses the illustration of a very small haulage business. It has one single asset, namely a vehicle valued at £20 000 that the owner uses to transport goods on a jobbing basis. The business has no inventories or accounts receivable, it has no bank or other loans and all its transactions are carried out for cash.

The simple opening balance sheet shows a single asset of £20 000 is represented by capital to the same amount. Beneath the opening balance sheet, the profit and loss account for the year is shown. The highlights are:

- sales of £30 000
- total costs of £27 000
- profit of £3000.

Finally, we see the closing balance sheet. It shows a cash figure of £8000. The company started with no cash and ended up with £8000, even though it made a profit of only £3000. How can this be?

The make-up of the final £8000 cash is shown to be:

- profit of £3000
- depreciation of £5000

The alternative way to view this is to look at the cash costs – £22 000 – and compare them with the cash revenue – £30 000. However, in most accounts, it is easier to go to the trading profit and add back the depreciation.

An interesting result of the depreciation effect is that there are certain types of companies that can suffer serious trading losses while maintaining adequate cash supplies. Many of these are in transportation, airlines, shipping, utilities and so on, where depreciation is a big percentage of total cost. So long as losses are less than the depreciation charged in the accounts, operations are cash positive.

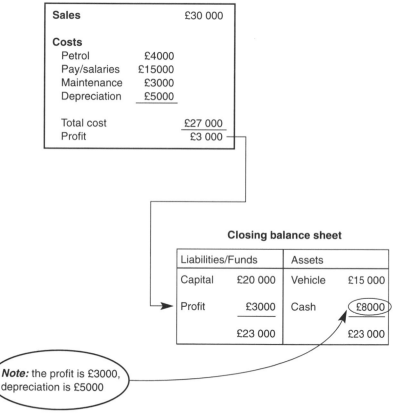

Opening balance sheet

Liabilities/Funds	Assets
Capital £20 000	Vehicle £20 000

Operating cash flow
=
Operating profit
+
Depreciation

(but see Appendix 1).

Profit and loss account

Sales		£30 000
Costs		
Petrol	£4000	
Pay/salaries	£15000	
Maintenance	£3000	
Depreciation	£5000	
Total cost		£27 000
Profit		£3 000

Closing balance sheet

Liabilities/Funds		Assets	
Capital	£20 000	Vehicle	£15 000
Profit	£3000	Cash	£8000
	£23 000		£23 000

Note: the profit is £3000, depreciation is £5000

Figure 8.3   Clarifying the relationships between depreciation and cash flow

Non-operating cash out-flows

Figures 8.1 and 8.2 show cash flowing round in a closed circuit. If there were no leaks from this circuit, there would be few problems. However, this is not the case and we must now add further sections to the diagram to allow for cash out-flows that are not related to day-to-day operations.

The main out-flows are shown in Figure 8.4 and are:

> - interest, tax and dividends
> - loan repayments
> - capital expenditure.

Interest, tax and dividends

These three items appear in the profit and loss account beneath the operating profit figure (profit before interest and tax). They are a distribution of some of the profit earned for the period. Probably 75 per cent of the profit in any year goes out under these headings. This leaves approximately 25 per cent that is permanently retained in the business. Furthermore, the profit is earned and realised in cash well ahead of these out-flows. If profit is low, then tax and dividends may also be reduced. So, this first set of payments should not, of themselves, be a major cause of cash embarrassment.

Loan repayments

These are usually substantial in amount. They are also deducted from after-tax income and are in no way connected with the profit for the period. However, the amounts required are known well in advance and, in most situations, can be planned and provided for.

Capital expenditure

This final item is nearly always a matter of policy. It can probably be deferred in unfavourable circumstances. It is subjected to much thought, analysis and planning. Nevertheless, heavy expenditure on projects that do not perform to plan is probably the major cause of cash difficulties.

The final piece of the diagram will be put in place next and we can then start to analyse the total picture.

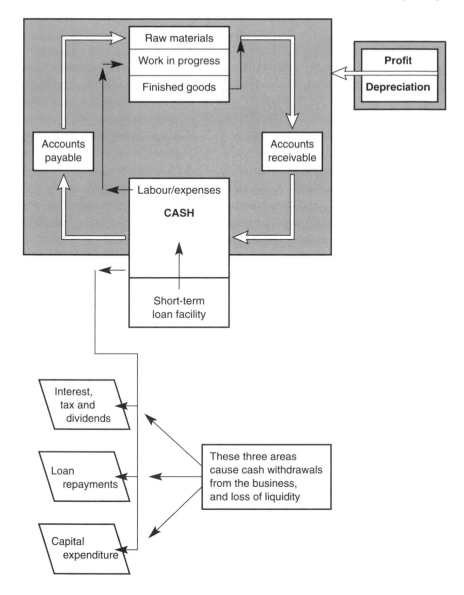

Figure 8.4 The main non-operating cash out-flows

Non-operating cash in-flows

In Figure 8.5, the right-hand final branch of the diagram has been completed. Three sources of cash from external sources are shown feeding into the diagram. These are:

- new equity capital
- new long-term loans
- sale of fixed assets.

In many parts of the world, a fourth source of cash is available in the form of grants from government to stimulate investment and employment, but note that this has been ignored here.

In raising long-term funds for a business, three matters must be given attention:

- cost
- risk
- control.

New equity capital
It is a function of the Stock Exchange to raise resources for commercial enterprises and there is a constant stream of public companies raising more cash from public or financial institutions. The great advantage of equity capital is that it is permanent and carries no risk. However, it is high-cost money and expensive in terms of control.

New long-term loans
Companies are continually repaying and raising long-term debts. It is the nature of banks to provide term loans for relatively short fixed periods. Companies *never* pay off their debts – they simply replace them with new debts. However, each time a company goes looking for new debts it must prove itself to be credit worthy; it must show strong evidence that it can service both the interest and principal. In many ways, debt has features that are the *opposite* of equity: it is less costly, it does not dilute control, but it brings extra risk.

Sale of fixed assets
This is not one commonly resorted to. However, it may be the only way out of a liquidity crisis. Indeed, sometimes it can be a very beneficial move at other times.

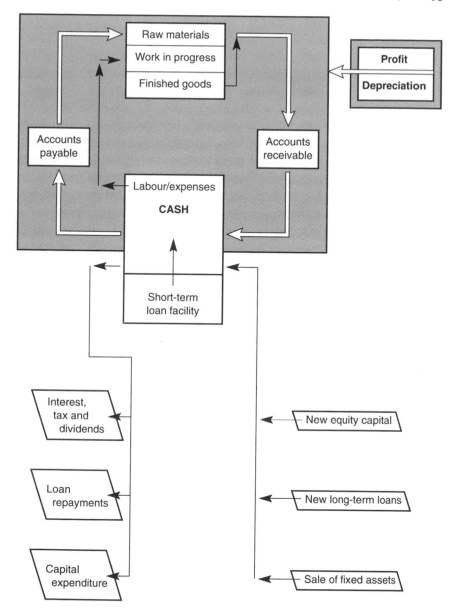

Figure 8.4 The main non-operating cash in-flows

MEASURES OF LIQUIDITY – LONG AND SHORT ANALYSIS

When we look at a company's liquidity position we must make a distinction between long- and short-term sections of the balance sheet. Figure 8.6 shows the five-box balance sheet and highlights these two areas.

Current assets and current libailities both fall into the short-term area, the remaining three boxes – ordinary funds, long term loans and fixed assets – into the long-term area. A certain balance should exist between the long-term assets and funds on the one hand and the short-term assets and funds on the other. As a general rule, long-term assets in a company should be matched by corresponding long-term liabilities and vice versa.

Company profiles

A balance sheet with its five boxes drawn to scale can highlight the profile of a company. By *profile* we mean the shape of the balance sheet in terms of the relative weight of each of the five boxes. These profiles are determined by the operating characteristics of the industrial sector in which a company operates.

Such profiles throw useful light on how a company will respond to certain conditions. Companies that are heavy in current assets will be adversely affected by an increase in the rate of inflation very quickly. Companies that have borrowed heavily are, of course, very responsive to changes in overall levels of interest rates.

Examples of two contrasting companies are shown in Figure 8.7. On the left we see the balance sheet outline of a company from the brewing sector. A very high percentage of the total assets are in the long-term investment area of fixed assets and there is a corresponding reliance on long term loans.

The balance sheet on the right-hand side represents a company from the textile sector. The heavy investment here is in short-term current assets and liabilities and we see that the mix of funds follows. We would expect this company to have more free borrowing from suppliers and, therefore, a lower overall cost of funds.

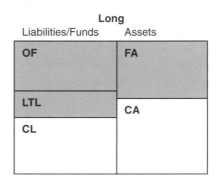

Figure 8.6 Long and short balance sheet analysis

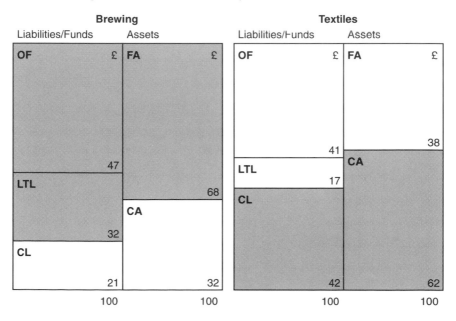

Figure 8.7 Long and short analysis of contrasting business sectors

9 LIQUIDITY

SHORT-TERM LIQUIDITY MEASURES

On first looking into a company's liquidity position, we concentrate on the short-term. We try to put a measure on the company's ability to provide cash to meet current liabilities as they fall due. These short-term liabilities amount to a considerable part of the total borrowings of the company. They are due to be paid in a relatively short time and are always greater than the company's pure cash resources. The question we ask is, 'Where will the cash come from to pay them?'

Cash is in constant movement through the company, flowing in principally from accounts receivable as we saw in Figure 8.2. Accounts receivable, in turn, is kept topped up from the finished goods inventory, which is fed by work in progress and so on. These are the assets that collectively make up current assets. At the same time, goods are being purchased on credit and other short-term loans are being taken out. These short-term assets and liabilities are in constant movement and the main measures of short-term liquidity concentrate on the relationship between the two values of current assets and current liabilities. Three ways of analysing this relationship are illustrated:

- current ratio
- quick ratio
- working capital to sales percentage.

The final ratio in this chapter is one that gives a more comprehensive view on the debt servicing capacity of a company, which is:

- interest cover.

Long-term measures of liquidity are given in Chapter 10.

CURRENT RATIO

The current ratio is a great favourite of banks. It is a simple comparison between the current assets and current liabilities. It can be expected that the current assets will be at least equal to, and, indeed, will normally be somewhat greater than, current liabilities. We therefore look for a value in excess of 1.0 for this ratio. However, certain types of companies are capable of operating with this ratio much less than 1.0.

In Figure 9.1 you can see that the average for the FT-SE Companies 1990 is 1.3 and that the variation for the 50 per cent range is evenly spread, plus or minus 0.3, making the range that of 1.0 to 1.6 times.

A word of caution is needed concerning the interpretation of this or any other ratio for a particular company. A wide diversity of conditions exist in different types of business, some businesses being able to exist comfortably with liquidity ratios that would spell disaster for others. Some companies have to carry large stocks, have long production cycles, give long credit and so on, while other businesses carry almost no stock and receive more credit than they give.

One ratio value in isolation, therefore, tells us little. A standard for comparison is needed. The standard can be derived from many sources, such as historical data and trends, competitors' accounts and published data of all kinds.

It can be said regarding liquidity ratios, that it is the trend over time that gives the most valuable information. A ratio value of 1.3 can, therefore, be either a good or bad signal. If it signalled a strong negative movement from the previous year it would be a bad signal and vice versa.

A disadvantage of this ratio is that it does not distinguish between different types of current assets, some of which are far more liquid than others. A company could be getting into cash problems and still have a strong current ratio.

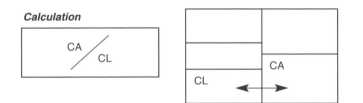

Balance sheet

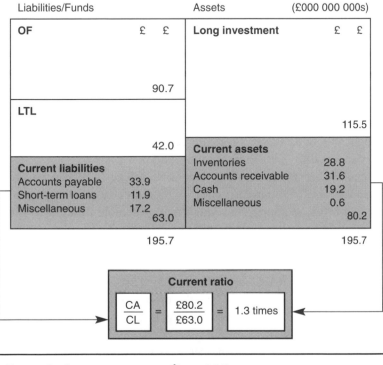

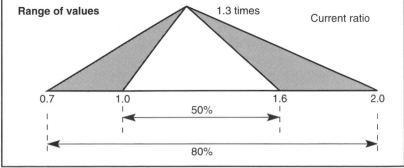

Figure 9.1 Current ratio applied to data from the FT-SE Companies 1990

Analysis by sectors using the current ratio

In Figure 9.2, most of the sectors show a close clustering of the current ratio around 1.3 times, with one sector a little high and another very low. Both give significant messages.

On the far right, the health sector has a value of 1.6. We saw in the debtor days calculation in Chapter 7 that extended credit to customers is normal in this sector. The high value of accounts receivable that results from this policy largely accounts for the high current assets figure. It is also a feature of this sector that many companies hold large amounts of cash in their balance sheet. They are highly liquid .

On the extreme left of the charts, the food retailing sector is in the opposite position. These companies have a current ratio of less than 0.5. The rule that the ratio should not be less than 1.0 mentioned earlier clearly does not apply here. If it applied universally, these companies should be extremely short of cash. However, the rule even though it works at a general level, is not applicable in *all* cases. There are certain types of companies that operate very successfully with current ratios well below unity.

In retailing, cash from trading comes in before it is paid out, but, for most businesses, the opposite occurs – they must pay cash to suppliers, for labour and other operating costs quite a considerable time before the cash comes back in from the customers. These companies have a *negative cash trading cycle*, whereas the food retailing sector includes businesses where the trading cash cycle is *positive*.

These companies purchase goods on Day 1, sell for cash on Day 7 and pay the supplier on Day 40. They therefore build up cash balances of roughly 30 days' purchases (we will see more of this at work under the quick ratio that follows).

There are other types of businesses where this type of cash flow occurs. Many small contracting or service-type businesses take money on deposit and deliver value later. Many such companies operate from extremely precarious cash positions and it is wise to be cautious in dealing with them.

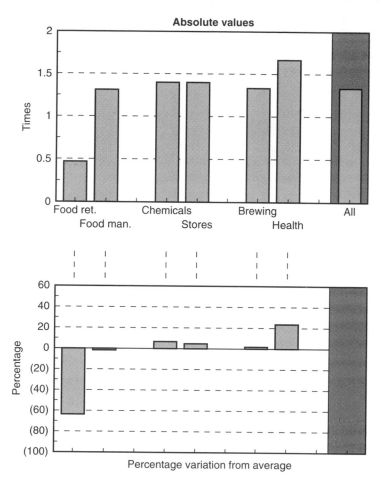

Figure 9.2 *Current ratio by sectors from FT-SE Companies 1990*

QUICK RATIO

This ratio is simply the current ratio with the inventories value removed from the current assets total. Figure 9.3 shows an average of 0.8 times with the 50 per cent range being from 0.7 to 1.1 times. A value of 1.0 is very strong and means that the company can pay off all its short-term liabilities from its cash balances plus its accounts receivable. This ratio is sometimes called the *acid test*.

The reason for excluding the inventory figure is that its liquidity can be a problem. You will recall that the term liquidity is used to express how quickly and to what percentage of its book value an asset can be converted into cash in a crisis. For instance, a cargo of high-quality crude oil docked at Rotterdam would have high liquidity, whereas a large stock of fashion garments would have a low one. We sometimes meet with a situation where we get a constant current but a falling quick ratio. It is a most dangerous sign. It tells us that stock is building up at the expense of receivables and cash. Banks and other lenders have difficulty is ascertaining the liquidity of many types of inventory. They feel much more comfortable when dealing with receivables and cash.

While both the current and quick ratios are the most widely used measures of short-term liquidity, they are static, looking at values at one time only, which is the balance sheet date. Many companies will try to create the best possible figures this one day only. It is argued that cash flow over the short-term future would be a better indicator of ability to pay. The working capital to sales ratio illustrated overleaf meets this objection to a certain extent.

Analysis by sectors using the quick ratio

We can see that the FT-SE Companies 1990 have large cash balances in the balance sheet amounting to 10 per cent of their total assets. This is an unusually high figure – 2 per cent is more common. These companies are, for the most part, very liquid, and we should allow for that in comparing them with other companies.

Balance sheet

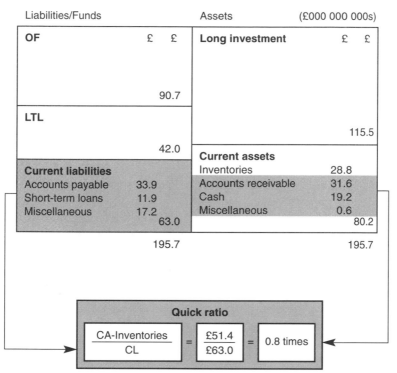

Liabilities/Funds			Assets		(£000 000 000s)
OF	£	£	**Long investment**	£	£
		90.7			
LTL					115.5
		42.0			
Current liabilities			**Current assets**		
			Inventories	28.8	
Accounts payable	33.9		Accounts receivable	31.6	
Short-term loans	11.9		Cash	19.2	
Miscellaneous	17.2		Miscellaneous	0.6	
		63.0			80.2
		195.7			195.7

Quick ratio

$$\frac{\text{CA-Inventories}}{\text{CL}} = \frac{£51.4}{£63.0} = 0.8 \text{ times}$$

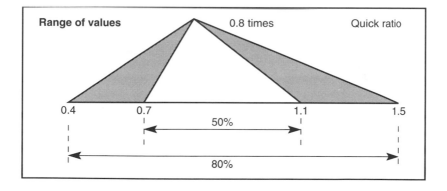

Range of values	0.8 times	Quick ratio

0.4   0.7   1.1   1.5

50%

80%

Figure 9.3 Quick ratio applied to data from the FT-SE Companies 1990

WORKING CAPITAL TO SALES RATIO

The ratio illustrated in Figure 9.4 gives us a glimpse of a company's short-term liquidity position from yet another angle. This ratio shows up some features that cannot be ascertained easily from the previous two.

In Chapter 1, working capital was defined as being current assets less current liabilities. This value is expressed here as a percentage of sales. Whereas the current and quick ratios look only at balance sheets figures, this one uses values from the profit and loss account too. The sales figure reflects, in some way, the operating cash flow through the whole system. This ratio, therefore, relates the surplus of short-term assets over short-term liabilities to the annual operating gross cash flow.

It will often highlight a trend the other ratios miss. It is possible to have a stable current or quick ratio while this ratio is falling. This will happen when sales are increasing rapidly and there are constant levels of working capital – a situation that leads to overtrading.

The term *overtrading* is used to describe a situation where the balance sheet does not have sufficient resources to carry the level of existing business. It arises in a company that has grown too fast from its base or that has been underfunded in the first place. The symptoms show up as a constant shortage of cash to meet day-to-day needs. Nevertheless the modern trend is towards a lower working capital to sales ratio, particularly in the form of much reduced inventories.

We can see from Figure 9.4 that the spread of values for the FT-SE Companies 1990 is wide, going from a negative 8 per cent to a positive 41 per cent. This high number is influenced by the fact that some large companies in our sample hold significant cash balances. This is not a feature that will be encountered in medium-sized companies as mentioned earlier.

Profit and loss account

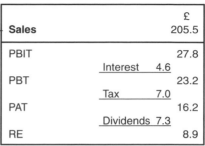

	£
Sales	205.5
PBIT	27.8
Interest 4.6	
PBT	23.2
Tax 7.0	
PAT	16.2
Dividends 7.3	
RE	8.9

Balance sheet

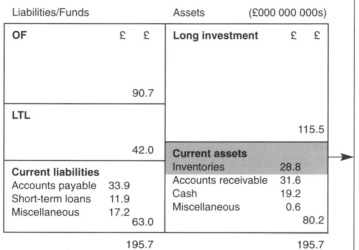

Liabilities/Funds			Assets	(£000 000 000s)	
OF	£	£	**Long investment**	£	£
		90.7			
LTL					115.5
		42.0			
Current liabilities			**Current assets**		
Accounts payable	33.9		Inventories	28.8	
Short-term loans	11.9		Accounts receivable	31.6	
Miscellaneous	17.2		Cash	19.2	
		63.0	Miscellaneous	0.6	
					80.2
		195.7			195.7

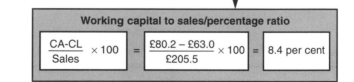

Working capital to sales/percentage ratio

$$\frac{CA-CL}{Sales} \times 100 = \frac{£80.2 - £63.0}{£205.5} \times 100 = 8.4 \text{ per cent}$$

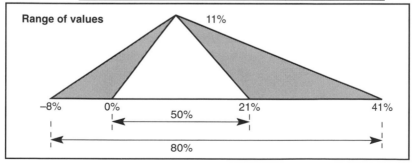

Range of values

11%

−8%   0%   21%   41%

50%

80%

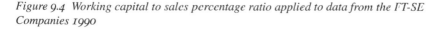

Figure 9.4 Working capital to sales percentage ratio applied to data from the FT-SE Companies 1990

INTEREST COVER

Here we have an important liquidity ratio of more recent vintage that gives us some supplementary information. It is unique in that it is the only one derived solely from the profit and loss account. The interest charged is divided into the profit before income tax figure to give the *cover,* expressed as so many *times.*

It is interesting to consider the difference between this and previous ratios. The interest charge in the accounts is determined by:

- the total borrowed and
- the effective rate of interest.

While the balance sheet ratios looked solely at the total borrowed, this ratio takes account of two factors not covered by them:

- the profitability of the company
- average interest rates.

A highly profitable company can have very adequate interest cover even though the balance sheet may appear to be over borrowed. Also, of course, large movements in the base interest levels in the economy will impact significantly on this ratio. This may partly explain why low interest economies seem to accept more highly leveraged balance sheets.

We can see in Figure 9.5 that the average for the FT-SE Companies 1990 is 6 times and the lower boundary for the 50 per cent central group of companies is 4.3 times. This latter value can be looked on as the lowest prudent level for a company. Except in unusual circumstances, very few companies operate with a level below 3 times.

The term *financial leverage* is used to reflect the relationship between profit and the fixed interest charge. If financial leverage is high, that is if interest is a high part of pre-interest profits, a small change in operating profit will be greatly magnified in its effect on return to the shareholders. A highly leveraged company does well in boom times, but quickly falls into difficulty in recession.

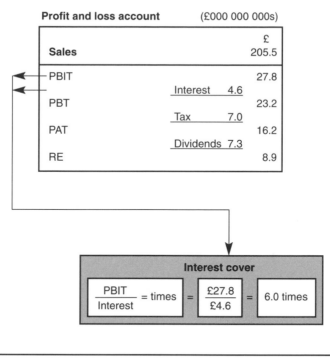

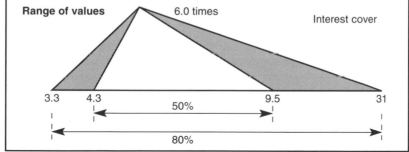

Figure 9.5 Interest cover applied to data from the FT-SE Companies 1990

DEBT TO EQUITY RATIO (D/E)

The debt to equity ratio is one of the most fundamental measures in corporate finance. It is the measure of the financial strength of a company. It is used universally, but, unfortunately, it turns up under so many different names and with so many different methods of calculation, that it gives rise to much confusion. The purpose of this ratio is to measure the mix of funds in the balance sheet and to draw a comparison between those funds that have been supplied by the owners (equity) and those which have been borrowed (debt). This distinction is illustrated in Figure 10.1.

The idea seems a very simple one, but, nevertheless, difficulties arise in two areas:

- 'What do we mean by debt?'
- 'How exactly will we express the calculation?'

First we will consider different possible interpretations of the term '*debt*'. Look at Figure 10.2 and you will see the three interpretations in common use:

- long-term loans only
- long- and short-term loans (including all interest-bearing debt)
- long-term loans plus all current liabilities.

Note that the first two definitions concentrate on *formal debt,* usually sourced from banks or other financial institutions. Therefore these definitions are often found in banks' calculations. The last definition includes trade creditors plus all accruals, such as dividends, tax and other miscellaneous amounts.

The reason bank analysts use the more restricted view of debt is understandable, given that they often stand ahead of trade and other creditors in the queue for payment. (Note that, at this point in the discussion, we are leaving out the important question of creditors with statutory preference.) From the banks' point of view the only debt that matters is that which ranks equal to or ahead of their own position. However, from the companies' viewpoint, debt due to a supplier is just as real and as important a debt as that due to a bank. There are therefore good arguments for including *all* debt in the calculation of the debt to equity ratio.

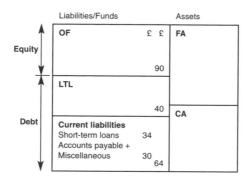

Figure 10.1 The debt to equity ratio

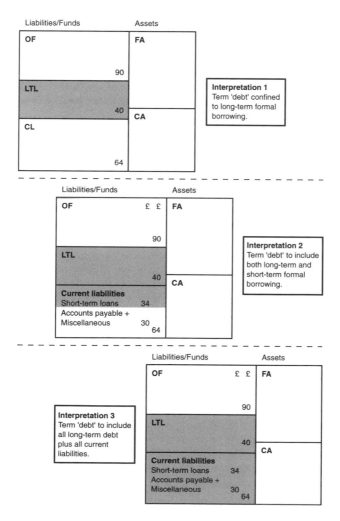

Figure 10.2 Interpretations of debt

Debt/equity – methods of calculation

From a management point of view, as stated previously one kind of debt is just as important as another. For that reason, we will use the broadest definition of debt – long-term loans plus current liabilities – for the remainder of this book. This done, we will examine the various ways in which the ratio can be calculated.

First it needs to be emphasised that it matters little which method of calculation we use: different methods simply give different numbers that mean the same thing. Just as we can express length in inches or centimetres and each will be a different number, so we can express the relationship between equity and debt in different ways and the *ratio* is the same irrespective of how it is expressed. This point is quite important, because, while there seem to be dozens of business ratios of all kinds, there are only a small number that are absolutely fundamental *and* different.

Figure 10.3, shows three methods for expressing the debt to equity ratio:

- *Method 1 – debt over equity* This is the classic approach and it is used widely (but a more restricted definition of debt may be used). When a debt to equity value is quoted for a company, then, in the absence of evidence to the contrary, it should be assumed that this method has been used to achieve it.
- *Method 2 – equity over total funds* An approach that is not so common. The answer is almost the reciprocal of the third method below, which is encountered much more often.
- *Method 3 – debt over total funds* This approach is favoured by the author. It gives an instant picture of the total balance sheet on the funds side. The numbers are easily extracted from the most complex set of accounts.

(The thorny question of how to treat deferred tax and other miscellaneous funds is being ignored for the present. While these items can give rise to nice academic debates, in practice they do not cause serious difficulties, being insignificant in terms of the total balance sheet – *see* Appendix 1.)

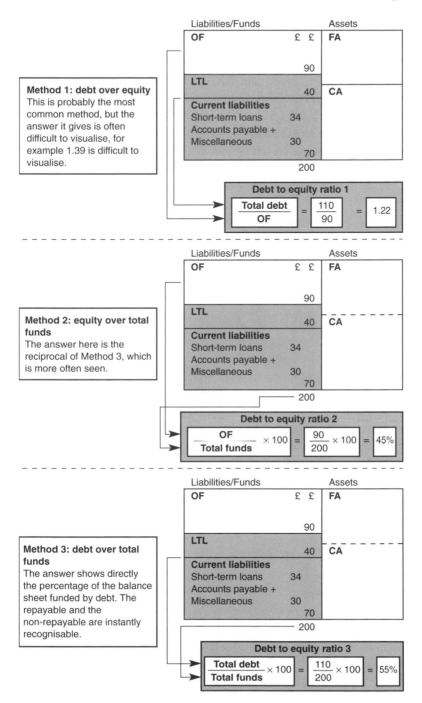

Figure 10.3 Different methods for expressing the debt into equity ratio

Debt/equity – why it is important

Much emphasis is placed on this ratio because, if it goes wrong, the company has a problem that will be very difficult to solve, indeed, it maybe terminal.

The greater the debt, the greater the risk. Debt in the balance sheet gives third parties legal claims on the company. These claims are for interest payments at regular intervals, plus repayment of the principal by the agreed time. This will be achieved either by periodic instalments or a single lump sum at the end of the loan period. When a company raises debt, it takes on a commitment to a substantial fixed cash out-flow for some time into the future. However, the company does not have a guaranteed cash in-flow over the same period. The in-flow may be most uncertain. With a fixed cash out-flow and an uncertain cash in-flow the company faces risk and so it follows that the greater is the sum to be paid out, the greater is the risk.

Why, then, do companies take on debt and incur this extra risk? The answer is that debt costs less than equity funds. By adding debt to its balance sheet, a company can generally improve its profitability, add to its share price, increase the wealth of its shareholders and develop greater potential for growth. Debt increases both profit *and* risk so a proper balance between these two factors has to be maintained.

Where should the line be drawn? We see from Figure 10.4 that the FT-SE Companies 1990 maintain approximately a one-to-one relationship between debt and equity. (Debt is almost 50 per cent of total assets). Likewise, in the US. However, in Figure 10.5 we can see that in Continental Europe, more than £2 debt for every £1 equity is common. In the Far East, the ratio can go above £5 debt for every £1 equity. Much has been written exploring the reasons for these variations and the general conclusion seems to be that they arise because of attitudinal, cultural and historical, rather than financial, factors.

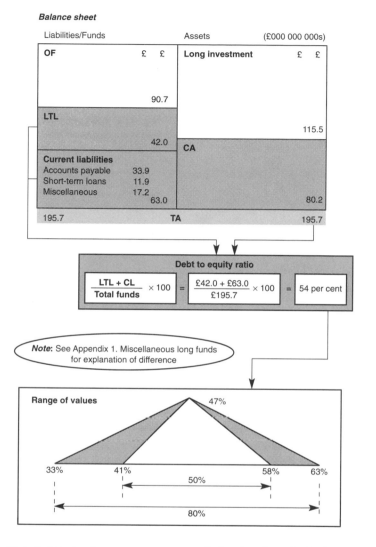

Figure 10.4 Debt to total assets percentage applied to data from the FT-SE Co. 1990

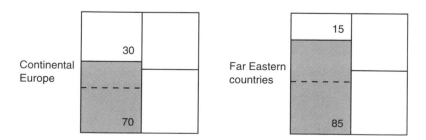

Figure 10.5 Patterns of debt to total assets levels in other parts of the world

Leverage

This subject is covered in greater depth in Chapter 13, but it is appropriate here to consider the impact of different debt to equity ratios on shareholders' returns. In Figure 10.6, Section A, we see a company for which the mix of funds has not yet been decided. It has assets of £100, sales of £120 and an operating profit of £15. The effects of different levels of gearing or leverage on the shareholders is illustrated in Sections B and C. (*Note*: For simplicity, tax is ignored and the interest rate is set at 10 per cent.)

In Section B, just one level of leverage is analysed to show you how the figures work. Option 1 in the first row illustrates a situation with £100 equity and no debt. There is, accordingly, no interest charge, so the total profit of £15 accrues to the shareholders' investment of £100. This gives a return to the shareholders of 15 per cent. In the second row, the mix has changed to £80 equity and £20 debt. The interest charge at 10 per cent is £2, which, deducted from the profit of £15, leaves £13 for the shareholders, whose investment is £80. The return of £13 on £80 gives the shareholders a 16.25 per cent return. As a result of introducing 20 per cent debt into the company, the return on equity ratio has increased from 15 per cent to 16.25 per cent. This is financial leverage in action.

In Section C, the leverage has been extended in steps all the way up to 90 per cent. With each additional slice of debt, the return on equity ratio increases until it reaches 60 per cent at the 90 per cent level of debt. Extraordinarily high levels of return can be achieved from very highly leveraged companies. The price that is paid for these high returns is the additional exposure to risk.

Apart from the geographical differences noted previously, some sectors of industry are traditionally highly leveraged. First we can ask what factors would encourage high borrowing. A very stable income is a most important factor. For example, to have good property on long lease to a secure tenant would signal a stable future income and such a proposal could, therefore, be very highly leveraged.

Section A

Balance sheet extract

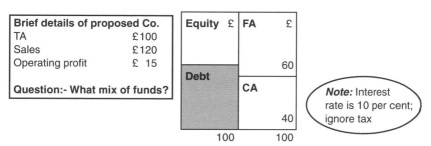

Brief details of proposed Co.	
TA	£100
Sales	£120
Operating profit	£ 15
Question:- What mix of funds?	

Note: Interest rate is 10 per cent; ignore tax

Section B

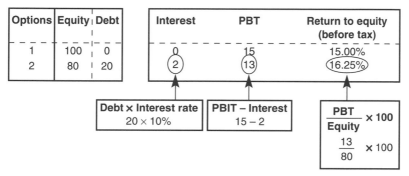

Section C

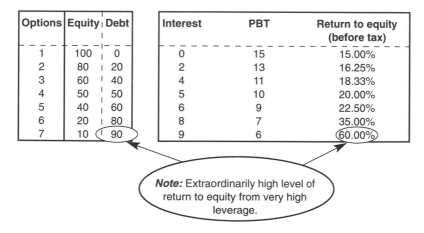

Note: Extraordinarily high level of return to equity from very high leverage.

Figure 10.6 Effects of different levels of leverage

11 CASH FLOW

CASH FLOW STATEMENTS

The third main item required to complete a company's set of published accounts is its cash flow statement. The profit and loss account uses the accruals concept to adjust a company's cash flows to bring them into line with revenue earned and costs incurred for a specific period. While it is most important that *true* revenue and costs are identified, the adjustments sometimes make it difficult to ascertain exactly *what* the overall company result was. The cash flow statement, particularly in its new format (*see* Figure 11.6, page 129) adds greatly to our information about the way in which a company has carried out its operations over the period covered by the accounts. Not only does it show the movements of cash, it is a very powerful tool for explaining what lies behind movements in the various liquidity ratios.

The cash flow statement has been presented in many formats, but it has now been standardised (as shown in simplified form in Figure 11.6). Its purpose is to track the flow of funds through the company. It identifies *how much* cash has flowed through the company's accounts, where it has *gone to* and where it has *come from*. Indeed, many would contend that the information in it is more reliable and less subject to manipulation than the profit and loss account.

The rules relating to cash flow are very simple. Every time a company writes a cheque, it has a cash out-flow. When a cheque is received, there is a cash in-flow. This is the *only* rule and its very simplicity means that it is difficult to find mechanisms to hide unpleasant truths. However, despite its clarity, it cannot, as is occasionally suggested, replace the profit and loss account. The latter correctly distinguishes between cash paid for electricity consumed last month and cash paid for a building that will be occupied by the company for the next 20 years.

This chapter looks at the different cash flow layouts that will be of use to management before illustrating the format of the most recent accounting standard.

SOURCES AND USES OF FUNDS – METHOD

To get at the data needed in order to build a cash flow statement, we go through a *sources and uses* exercise. The mechanics of this exercise are easy to grasp and are shown in Figure 11.1 opposite.

A complete but simplified balance sheet is shown for the two years 1993 and 1994. It has been laid out in vertical columns to facilitate comparison between the two years. The assets are in the upper section of the statement and the liabilities in the lower. To the right of the balance sheet, two extra columns have been added – respectively *source* and *use*. An entry will be made in one of these columns for every *change* that has taken place in a balance sheet item.

If the change has caused a cash *out-flow*, the entry will be entered in the *use* column. For a cash *in-flow*, the entry will be made in the *source* column.

Two entries have been illustrated:

1 Fixed assets – out-flow of £10,000   – use
2 Tax   – in-flow of   £500   – source

The logic of the first entry is fairly obvious. To increase the value of the fixed asset from £22,500 to £32,500, the company has had to write a cheque for £10,000. (For the purposes of this exercise we ignore revaluation and depreciation – *see* Appendix 1.)

The second entry is less obvious. How can an increase in *tax* be a source of *funds*? The answer is that the tax amount of £3000 shown as a liability in the closing balance sheet is unpaid. The company now has the use of £500 *more* government money than it had one year ago. This liability will have to be paid off in due course. It will then disappear from the balance sheet and be picked up as a use of funds.

The completed statement and the logic behind it is shown overleaf.

Balance sheets (£000s)	1993 £	1994 £	Source £	Use £
Assets				
Fixed assets	22 500	32 500		10 000
Current assets				
Inventories (stocks)	12 500	14 350		
Accounts receivable (debtors)	15 000	16 000		
Cash	1750	0		
Total assets	51 750	62 850		
Liabilities				
Issued capital	18 000	18 000		
Reserves	9500	10 750		
Long-term loans	8000	9000		
Current liabilities				
Accounts payable (creditors)	13 750	17 000		
Short-term loans	0	5100		
Current tax due	2500	3000	500	
Total liabilities	51 750	62 850		

Note:
Increase in liability
=
source of funds

Note:
Increase in assets
=
use of funds

Figure 11.1 Sources and uses of funds – examples

Rules of construction

The full statement is shown in Figure 11.2. All movements have been identified and classified into their correct columns; the totals of the two columns
agree (the sources and uses *must* balance once changes in the short-term
cash position have been allowed for).

At first it is easy to get the source and use items the wrong way round,
but there is a rule that makes the classification very simple:

Asset	Increase............	Use
	Decrease	Source
Liability	Increase............	Source
	Decrease	Use.

For each change in a balance sheet value, the following questions need to
be asked:

- 'Is the item an asset or liability?'
- 'Has it increased or decreased?'

then the item automatically slots into its correct column.

The exercise illustrates a technique that allows us to translate all changes
in balance sheet values into corresponding movements of funds. The method
demonstrated is called the *indirect method.* Instead of picking up *all* cash
flow, such as payments to suppliers and receipts from customers (the *direct
method*), only the movement in the closing balances is identified, which is
sufficient for our purposes.

Hidden movements

A word of caution is needed here. The indirect method picks up net movements *only* in balance sheet values. A net change can, of course, be the
result of two opposite movements that partly cancel one another out. Also,
some movements in balance sheet values do not give rise to cash flow –
revaluation of fixed assets for example, (*see* Appendix 1). It may be necessary to get behind some of the numbers to find out if there are any hidden
movements. Notwithstanding these qualifications, the method is a powerful
tool of analysis.

Balance sheets (£000s)	1993 £	1994 £	Source £	Use £
Assets				
Fixed assets	22 500	32 500		10 000
Current assets				
Inventories (stocks)	12 500	14 350		1850
Accounts receivable (debtors)	15 000	16 000		1000
Cash	1750	0	1750	
Total assets	51 750	62 850		
Liabilities				
Issued capital	18 000	18 000		
Reserves	9500	10 750	1250	
Long-term loans	8000	9000	1000	
Current liabilities				
Accounts payable (creditors)	13 750	17 000	3250	
Short-term loans	0	5100	5100	
Current tax due	2500	3000	500	
Total liabilities	51 750	62 850	12 850	12 850

Hidden movements
This figure gives the net change in fixed assets.
It probably masks a depreciation charge counterbalanced
by an even greater figure for new investment, for example
if depreciation of £2500 had been charged in the period,
then the total new investment is £12 500.
Both sources and uses totals are increased by £2500.

Figure 11.2 Completed allocation of sources and uses of funds

OPENING AND CLOSING CASH RECONCILIATION

Once the sources and uses have been identified and reconciled, we can use various layouts to give management information about different aspects of the company. For instance, the company's cash position at the start plus the net cash flow over the period in question should equal its closing cash position. The layout shown in Figure 11.3 illustrates such a reconciliation. (*Note*: The day-to-day cash balance can be positive *or* negative. A positive position is where there is cash at bank whereas a negative position shows up as short-term bank loan.)

With the exceptions of movements in cash and short-term bank loans, all the items in the use column are listed under cash-out. Items in the source column are listed under cash-in.

The total for cash-out comes to £12 850. The total for cash-in comes to £6000. The net cash flow is the difference – £6850 (negative). This value, added to the opening cash figure of £1750 gives the closing cash position of £5100 (negative).

This statement shows the overall cash reconciliation and it also explains any large changes in the cash position. Even a cursory examination of the cash-out and cash-in items shows the *reason* for the negative cash flow. The company has *expended* £10 000 on fixed assets. This relatively large sum has not been *matched* by any corresponding large cash *in-flow*. The assets have been purchased from day-to-day operating cash.

The heavily negative net cash flow also helps to explain why the current ratio for the company has dropped from 1.8 to 1.2 times between 1993 and 1994 and the debt to total assets ratio has increased from 47 per cent to 54 per cent. This aspect is pursued overleaf.

Balance sheets (£000s)	1993 £	1994 £	Source £	Use £
Assets				
Fixed assets	22 500	32 500		10 000
Current assets				
Inventories (stocks)	12 500	14 350		1850
Accounts receivable (debtors)	15 000	16 000		1000
Cash	1750	0	1750	
Total assets	51 750	62 850		
Liabilities				
Issued capital	18 000	18 000		
Reserves	9500	10750	1250	
Long-term loans	8000	9000	1000	
Current liabilities				
Accounts payable (creditors)	13 750	17 000	3250	
Short-term loans	0	5100	5100	
Current tax due	2500	3000	500	
Total liabilities	51 750	62 850	12 850	12 850

Current ratio   1.8   1.2 times
Debt/total assets   46 per cent 54 per cent

Opening cash position (A)   £1750

    Cash out (uses)   £   £
    Fixed assets   (10 000)
    Inventories   (1850)
    Accounts receivable   (1000)
      B) Total cash out   (12 850)

    Cash in (sources)
    Reserves   1250
    Long-term loans   1000
    Accounts payable   3250
    Current tax due   500
      C) Total cash in   6000

    D) Net cash flow (C-B)   (£6850)

Closing cash position (A-D)   (£5100)

Figure 11.3 Opening and closing cash reconciliation

LONG AND SHORT ANALYSIS

The information provided in Figure 11.3 adds considerably to our previous knowledge of the company's affairs derived from the balance sheet and profit and loss account. Alternative layouts of the cash flow data can provide even more insights.

In Figure 11.4, the same original data has been plotted into a grid that distinguishes between long- and short-term sources on the one hand and long- and short-term uses on the other (refer back to page 95 where the long- and short-term sections of the balance sheet were identified).

Each item in the source column has been identified as either long- or short-term and put into the appropriate box. All the items in the use column have been treated likewise. The separate sections of the grid are totalled to give four major values for compaison with one another.

The main expenditure has taken place in the long-term area. We can trace the purchase of a large fixed assets for £10,000 into this box. The corresponding box containing long-term source funds falls considerably short at £2250. We know that the long-term funds sections of the balance sheet are the ordinary funds box and the long-term loan box and the amounts secured under both of these headings are low.

The large sums are in the short-term box on the sources side. Most of the money that has come into the business has come from accounts payable and bank overdraft. This means that they will have to be repaid within 12 months. We have already seen that both the current and debt to total assets ratios show a sharp disimprovement over the 1993-1994 period. These grid totals (which are analysed overleaf in further detail) throw light on movements in the liquidity position.

Long and short analysis

Balance sheets (£000s)	1993 £	1994 £	Source £	Use £
Assets				
Fixed assets	22 500	32 500		10 000
Current assets				
Inventories (stocks)	12 500	14 350		1850
Accounts receivable (debtors)	15 000	16 000		1000
Cash	1750	0	1750	
Total assets	51 750	62 850		
Liabilities				
Issued capital	18 000	18 000		
Reserves	9500	10 750	1250	
Long-term loans	8000	9000	1000	
Current liabilities				
Accounts payable (creditors)	13 750	17 000	3250	
Short-term loans	0	5100	5100	
Current tax due	2500	3000	500	
Total liabilities	51 750	62 850	12 850	12 850

	Source		Use	
		£		
Long	Reserves	1250	Fixed assets	10 000
	Long-term loans	1000		
		2250		10 000
Short	Accounts payable	3250	Inventories	1850
	Short-term loans	5100	Accounts receivable	1000
	Cash	1750		
	Current tax due	500		
		10 600		2850
		12 850		12 850

Figure 11.4 Long and short analysis of sources and uses of funds

Long and short strategy

In Figure 11.5, the long and short grid of Figure 11.4 is repeated, but the detail has been removed to leave only the total values in each section. Arrows show the movements of funds. The largest single movement of funds in the company for the 1993-1994 period has been the £7750 raised short and invested long.

The problem with this strategy is that the short-term funds will have to be repaid *quickly*, but they will not be *available* from the investment to meet this repayment. The company, therefore, can meet the repayments *only* from new funds raised at the time. No one can foretell what conditions will be like, either in the company or the money markets, when this need arises.

The grid has shown up a high-risk movement of funds. If the company cannot raise new funds to repay the short-term borrowing as it falls due, then it will have a serious liquidity problem. A well-known principle of finance is that funds for long-term uses should come from long-term sources – the matching principle. Short-term uses can be largely funded from short-term sources, but not entirely as we shall see.

A second rule to be observed is that the new funds into the company should come from a mix of sources in the proportions of a good debt to equity ratio. For example, if the company had an existing ratio of 60 per cent debt and 40 per cent equity, then we would expect the new funds to reflect, approximately, this same mix. In the example used, however, the funds have been raised as approximately 90 per cent debt (£11 600) and 10 per cent equity (£1250). This high level of debt in the new funds has, of course, damaged the overall debt to equity ratio of the company.

The final rule it is advisable to apply is that, to preserve the existing current ratio, the totals in the two short-term boxes should have the same relationship as current assets to current liabilities in the opening balance sheet. The short sources box should have a total of a little over 50 per cent of the short-uses box, instead of which it has approximately 700 per cent.

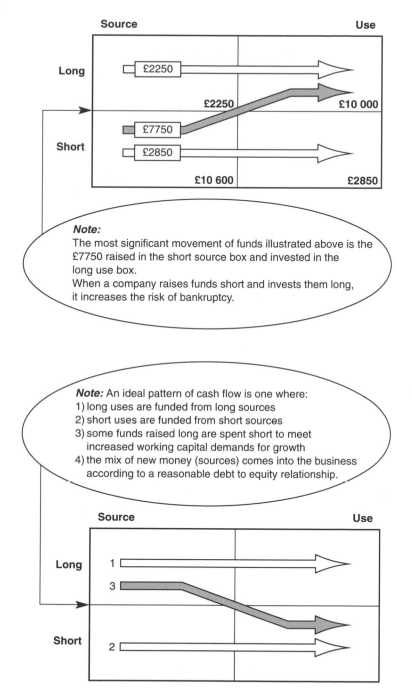

Figure II.5 Strategy for long and short movements of funds

FINANCIAL REPORTING STANDARD 1

The Accounting Standards Board (ASB) issued its first Financial Reporting Standard (FRS 1) on cash flow Statements in September 1991. It is a comprehensive and detailed document, the purpose of which is to lay down standards to give users information on the 'liquidity, viability and financial adaptability of the entity concerned'. This will be achieved by an improved understanding of a 'reporting entity's cash generating or cash absorption mechanisms' and will provide a 'basis for the assessment of future cash flow'.

In Figure 11.6 the author's approach to reconciling the explanatory cash flow illustrations used so far in this book is shown together with the main proposals given in the Standard. The Standard lays great stress on identifying the following separate components of the flow of cash and its equivalents:

- operating activities
- servicing of finance
- taxation
- investing activities
- financing activities.

It further requires a reconciliation of the figure shown for operating profit and operating cash flow, as well as a total showing the net cash in-flow or out-flow before financing.

Figure 11.6 identifies the main headings but omits much of the detail in the interest of clarity. The terminology in the reporting Standard will be widely used in boardrooms and management meetings over the coming years. It is important that managers be familiar with this terminology and appreciate the significance of the various components of cash flow. The sources and uses statement has been dropped as a reporting requirement, but it still remains a powerful tool of analysis for managers to use for their own benefit.

OPERATING ACTIVITIES

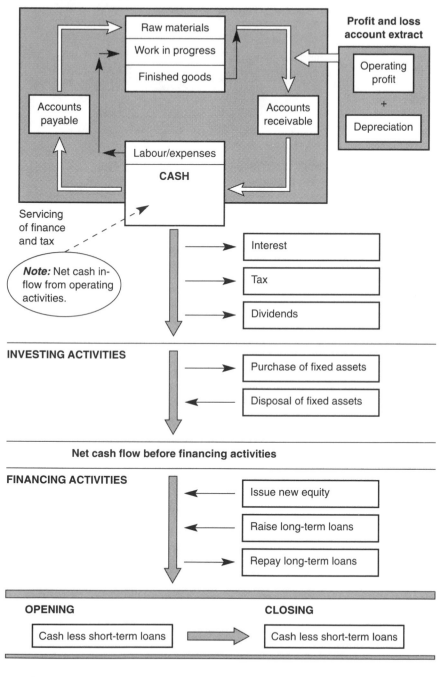

Figure 11.6 New format for cash flow statements related to Financial Reporting Standard 1

Part IV

DETERMINANTS OF
CORPORATE VALUE

12 CORPORATE VALUATION

INTRODUCTION

Public companies are valued by the stock market. Companies that are not publicly quoted will still have their value greatly influenced by the same market. In this chapter, therefore, we will look at the main stock market-related ratios. These are:

- market capitalisation
- share values, nominal, book, market
- earnings per share (EPS)
- dividends per share (DPS)
- dividend cover and the pay-out ratio
- earnings yield
- dividend yield
- price to earnings ratio (PE)
- market to book ratio.

When we talk about the value of a company we mean its market capitalisation or the combined value of the ordinary shares. We have already looked at the position that ordinary shares occupy in the balance sheet (*see* page 18). We have seen where they stand in the queue for participation in profits (*see* page 33). Both these issues are important for an understanding of this chapter.

In Figure 12.1 we again see the balance sheet for the Example Co. PLC. The top left-hand box shows ordinary funds totalling £360. This is the accounting approach. An alternative view of ordinary funds is to take the total assets figure of £800 and deduct from it the total loans figure of £440 (£200 + £240). This approach emphasises the importance of the asset values in determining shareholders' funds. Some adjustments to assets values (and, possibly, liabilities) might be necessary. The more likely areas are fixed assets, inventories and certain liabilities.

Balance sheet

Liabilities/Funds			Assets		(£000 000s)

Ordinary funds	£	£	Fixed assets	£	£
Issued ordinary shares	80		Intangibles	0	
Capital reserves	60		Net fixed assets	440	
Revenue reserves	220		Long-term investments	40	
		360			
LTL					480
		200	**Current assets**		
Current liabilities			Inventories	128	
Accounts payable	140		Accounts receivable	160	
Short-term loans	60		Cash	20	
Miscellaneous	40		Miscellaneous	12	
		240			320
		800			800

While *all* asset values can be queried and one or two liabilities, the main areas where difficulties can be expected are as follows.

Fixed assets How realistic are the values? We are primarily interested in value-in-use, but there are occasions when break-up value is important.

Inventories These very often present difficulty in determining the appropriate value. When we place a value on inventories we are making a judgement about future trading conditions. We are assuming that the value shown will be realised.

Liabilities There may be liabilities or potential liabilities that have not been provided for, such as pension liabilities not being fully funded.

Figure 12.1 Company valuation applied to data from the Example Co. PLC

SHARE VALUES

In Chapter 2, three types of share value were mentioned and we now look at these again in relation to the Example Co. PLC in Figure 12.2. There are 320 million issued ordinary shares, for each of which there is a:

Nominal	Value of	£0.25p
Book	Value of	£1.12
Market	Value of	£2.25.

Let us now look at each of these in turn.

Nominal value

The nominal value is largely a notional figure, but, when applied to the total number of issued shares of 320m, it gives the value for the issued 'ordinary shares'of £80m. If new shares are issued, they will hold this same nominal value even though the issue price will be much above it, probably close to the current market price. Say new shares go out at a price of £1.75, there is a surplus of £1.50 over the nominal value. This surplus is called the *share premium* and it forms part of the capital reserves.

Book value, or asset value, or asset backing

This value is calculated by taking the total for ordinary funds of £360m and dividing it by the number of issued shares – 320m. You will recall that we discussed the need to validate that sum of £360m. If an examination of the inventories produced a more prudent valuation of £20m down on the balance sheet value (£108m), this write-down would reduce the ordinary funds from £360m to £340m. The book value of the share would, therefore, fall from £1.12 to £1.06.

Market value

This is the price quoted in the Stock Exchange for a public company or an estimated price for a non-quoted company. On the Stock Exchange the figure changes daily in response to actual or anticipated results and overall or sectoral sentiment of the investors as reflected in the FT-SE indices. It can be argued that a main objective of management is to secure the best price possible under any set of conditions.

These different values will be used to derive the various ratios explored in the rest of this chapter.

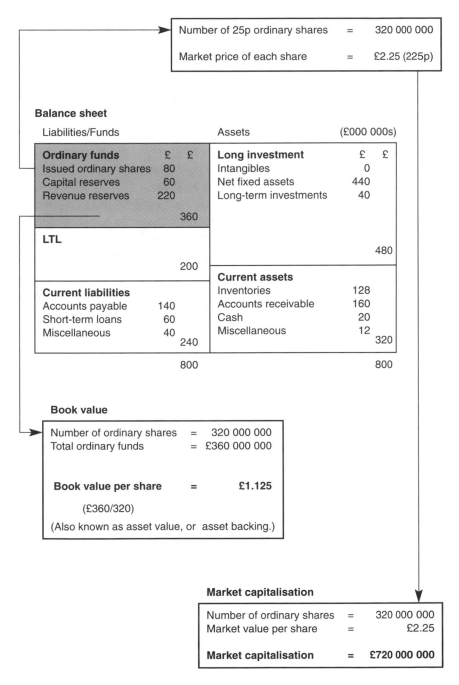

| Number of 25p ordinary shares | = | 320 000 000 |
| Market price of each share | = | £2.25 (225p) |

Balance sheet

| Liabilities/Funds | | | Assets | | (£000 000s) |

Ordinary funds	£	£	**Long investment**	£	£
Issued ordinary shares	80		Intangibles	0	
Capital reserves	60		Net fixed assets	440	
Revenue reserves	220		Long-term investments	40	
		360			480

LTL   200

Current liabilities			**Current assets**		
Accounts payable	140		Inventories	128	
Short-term loans	60		Accounts receivable	160	
Miscellaneous	40	240	Cash	20	
			Miscellaneous	12	320

| | | 800 | | | 800 |

Book value

| Number of ordinary shares | = | 320 000 000 |
| Total ordinary funds | = | £360 000 000 |

| **Book value per share** | = | **£1.125** |

(£360/320)

(Also known as asset value, or asset backing.)

Market capitalisation

| Number of ordinary shares | = | 320 000 000 |
| Market value per share | = | £2.25 |

| **Market capitalisation** | = | **£720 000 000** |

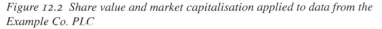

Figure 12.2 Share value and market capitalisation applied to data from the Example Co. PLC

Earnings per share (EPS)

Earnings per share is one of the most widely quoted statistics in discussion of a company's performance and share value.

Figure 12.3 shows how this ratio is calculated. Remember that the ordinary shareholder comes last in the queue for participating in profit. Used in this calculation, therefore, is the profit figure after all other claimants have been satisfied. The most common prior charges in the profit and loss account are interest and tax.

Therefore it is the profit after tax (PAT) figure in the profit and loss account that is divided by the number of ordinary shares to calculate the value of earnings per share. This figure tells us what profit has been earned by the ordinary shareholder for every share held.

It serves no purpose to compare the earnings per share in one company with that in another because a company can elect to have a large number of shares of low denomination or a smaller number of a higher denomination. A company can also decide to double the number of shares on issue and this decision will automatically reduce the earnings per share by 50 per cent. We cannot say, therefore, that a company with an earnings per share value of 50p is any better than one with a value of 40p.

While the absolute amount of earnings per share tells nothing about a company's performance, the growth in values over time is a very important statistic. Indeed, many chairpersons stress it as a target in the annual report. Furthermore, growth in earnings per share has a significant influence on the market price of the share.

Growth in earnings per share is used in preference to growth in absolute profit when assessing a company's progress. The reason is that growth in profits can result from a great many things. For instance, a company could acquire another for shares and thereby increase its profit. However, if the percentage increase in profit is less than the percentage increase in the number of shares, earnings per share will fall and the shareholders will lose out.

Not only is growth in earnings per share most important, so also is its stability. Investors look not only at absolute earnings but also at the quality of these earnings. A high quality rating is given to earnings that are showing steady non-volatile growth.

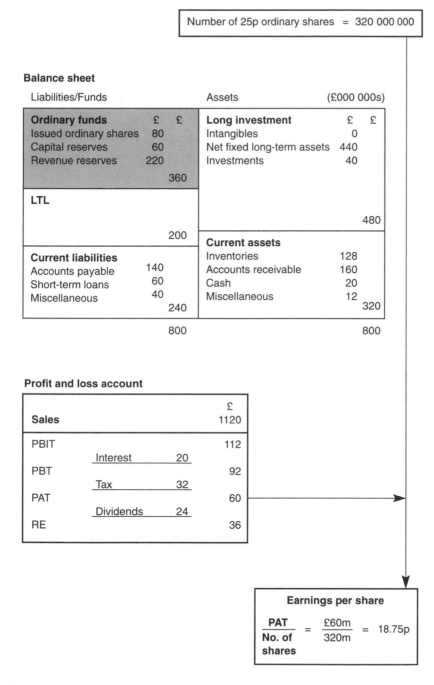

Figure 12.3 Earnings per share for the Example Co. PLC

Dividends per share

Figure 12.4 shows how to calculate this value. Of the earnings remaining in the profit and loss account for the shareholders' benefit only a certain fraction, at the discretion of the directors, is paid out to them in cash; the rest is retained to consolidate and expand the business.

It is a well-established rule that dividends are paid only out of *profits*, not from any other source. However, the earnings need not necessarily fall into the same year as the dividends. Thus situations arise when dividends exceed earnings. In such cases, dividends are being paid from earnings that have been retained in the business from previous years.

The total return from a share consists of the dividend received plus the growth in the share price over any given time. While, for some investors, growth is most important, many shareholders and potential investors pay very close attention to dividends. These are both private individuals and institutions such as pension fund investors who need income for their day-to-day affairs. They look at the absolute dividend per share and for a history of stable but growing payments.

Companies, therefore, intensely dislike being forced to reduce the dividend. Investors will, inevitably, be driven away from the shares, with possibly serious effects on their price. Accordingly, a company may decide that it must pay a dividend in excess of earnings rather than cut the pay-out. Of course, this is a policy that can be followed only for a short time and when there is reason to believe that earnings will recover to a figure greater than the dividends.

In the UK dividends received normally carry a tax credit because the company is obliged to pay Advance Corporation Tax (ACT) at the time the dividends are paid. We, therefore, come across the terms gross and net dividends. The net figure relates to the cash received. The gross figure is the amount that will be included in the recipients's statement of taxable income.

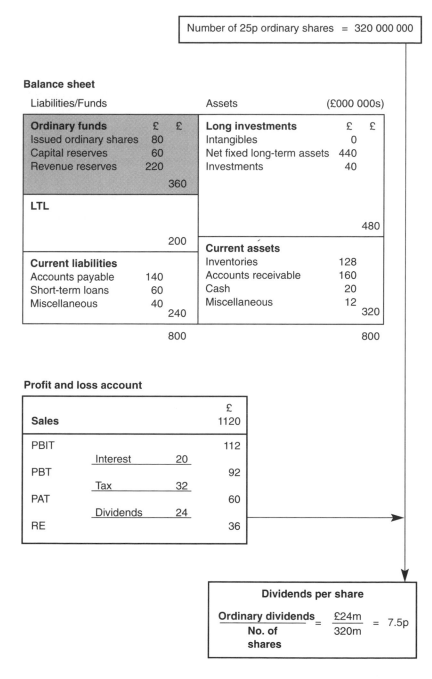

Figure 12.4 Dividends per share for the Example Co. PLC

Dividends cover and the pay-out ratio

These two ratios give the same information. They are simply reciprocals, that is mirror images, of each other. For the first ratio, divide earnings per share by dividends per share. For the second, reverse the numbers.*
Both identify the relationship between company earnings and cash paid out. Figure 12.5 shows the calculations of both.

We expect different cover values for different types of business. Public utility companies were noted for a high, stable pay-out policy and were, therefore, very popular with investors who needed income. On the other hand, some computer companies have never paid a dividend, even though they have made large profits over many years.

The importance of the dividend's cover is the indication it gives of the future stability and growth of the dividend:

- a high cover suggests that the dividend is fairly safe, because any expected downturn in profit will still leave the dividend well covered.
- a high cover (low pay-out ratio) also indicates a high retention policy, which suggests that the company is going for high growth.

Cover by sector and the FT-SE companies 1990
Figures 12.6 and 12.7 overleaf show what level of cover is normal. The combined accounts of the companies produce a value of 2.5 times for dividend cover (equal to a 40 per cent pay-out ratio). The sectoral analysis charts show how closely these particular sectors cluster around the average. The range of values chart shows that very few companies fall below a cover of 2 times.

It is worth while considering the implication of these numbers. Companies in the main retain more profits than they distribute. More than 50 per cent of equity returns, therefore, should come from capital growth, not dividends. However, capital growth depends on the share price. Share prices of all companies are quite volatile as can be tracked by movements in the FT-SE indices.

*These calculations use the earnings and dividend for a single share to arrive at the results. We can also use the earnings and dividend for the total company to derive the same results, as has been done for the FT-SE companies overleaf.

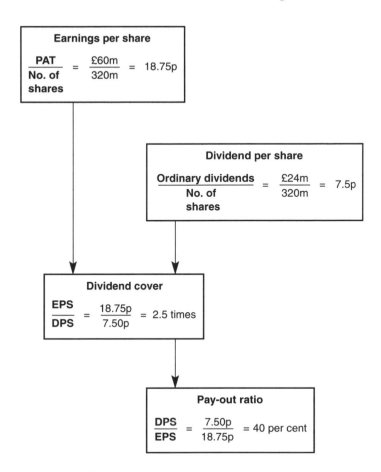

Figure 12.5 Dividends cover and the pay-out ratio for the Example Co. PLC

Balance sheet

Liabilities/Funds   Assets   (£000 000 000s)

Ordinary funds	£	£	**Long investments**	£	£
Issued ordinary shares	19.2		Intangibles	5.5	
Capital reserves	8.8		Net fixed assets	96.0	
Revenue reserves	62.7		Long-term investments	14.0	
		90.7			
LTL					115.5
		42.0			
			Current assets		
Current liabilities			Inventories	28.8	
Accounts payable	33.9		Accounts receivable	31.6	
Short-term loans	11.9		Cash	19.2	
Miscellaneous	17.2		Miscellaneous	0.6	
		63.0			80.2
		195.7			**195.7**

Profit and loss account

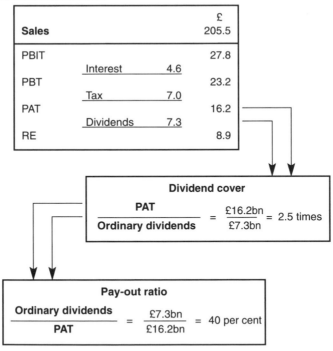

		£
Sales		205.5
PBIT		27.8
	Interest 4.6	
PBT		23.2
	Tax 7.0	
PAT		16.2
	Dividends 7.3	
RE		8.9

Dividend cover

$$\frac{\text{PAT}}{\text{Ordinary dividends}} = \frac{£16.2bn}{£7.3bn} = 2.5 \text{ times}$$

Pay-out ratio

$$\frac{\text{Ordinary dividends}}{\text{PAT}} = \frac{£7.3bn}{£16.2bn} = 40 \text{ per cent}$$

Figure 12.6 Dividends cover and the pay-out ratio for the FT-SE Companies 1990

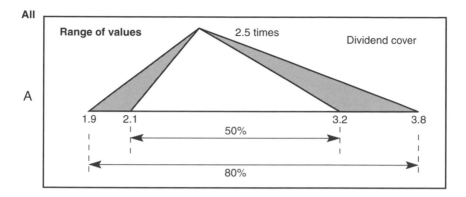

All

Range of values   2.5 times

Dividend cover

A

1.9   2.1   3.2   3.8

50%

80%

By sectors

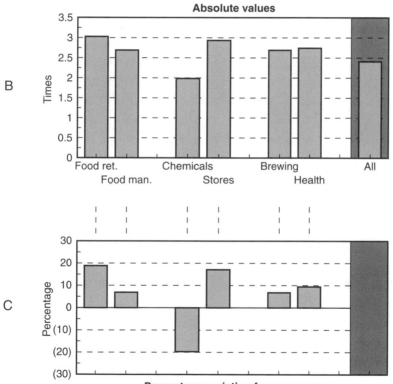

Absolute values

B

Times

3.5
3
2.5
2
1.5
1
0.5
0

Food ret.   Chemicals   Brewing   All
    Food man.   Stores   Health

C

Percentage

30
20
10
0
(10)
(20)
(30)

Percentage variation from average

Figure 12.7 Dividends cover by sector for the FT-SE Companies 1990

Share yield ratios

The yield on a share expresses the return to the shareholder as a percentage of the current share price. This calculation is used in respect of both earnings and dividends. Figure 12.8 shows both the earnings yield and the dividend yield calculations.

The earnings yield is a most important ratio. It moves down when the share price increases and vice versa. As the share price is controlled by the market the earnings yield represents the rate of return demanded by the investing community from the company. (We will use the letter 'K' to represent the value when we refer to it again in Chapter 13.)

Yield calculations allow useful comparisons to be made between the return on shares and other types of investment, such as government stocks (gilts) or commercial property. The effect of changes in the yield on security prices is a fundamental matter for the investor. The price of a security falls when the yield rises and vice versa. Managers of large investment funds constantly balance their portfolios of investment between these different investment outlets. In doing so, they must take account of yields, stability and capital growth expected in each area. We can look on the earnings yield on a company's shares as the cost to the company of attracting investors. Highly favoured companies show low yield values.

Yield by sector and the FT-SE Companies 1990
From the range of values chart, in Figure 12.8, it can be seen that for the FT-SE Companies 1990 earnings yields averaged 9% and dividend yields tended to cluster around 3 per cent to 5 per cent. These overall yields are inversely related to the level of the FT-SE 100 Share Index level, which stood at approximately 2100 when these values were calculated.

These yield values look low in comparison to gilt yields. The expression *reverse yield gap* is used to highlight the shortfall in dividend yields as opposed to those for gilts.

Note that yields quoted here are calculated net of tax. Both earnings and dividends yields as published are grossed up in the UK to incorporate the accompanying tax credit.

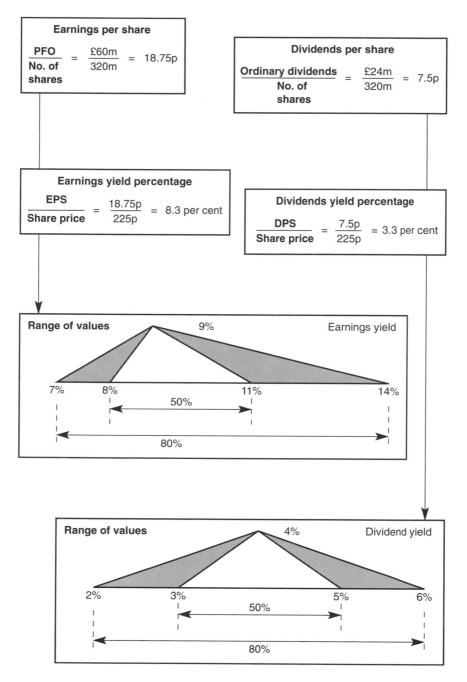

Figure 12.8 Share yield calculations for the Example Co. PLC and ranges for FT-SE companies

Price to earnings ratio

The price to earnings ratio or 'multiple' is a widely quoted parameter of share performance. Figure 12.9 shows the method of calculation. The share price is divided by the earnings per share figure. The answer gives the number of years' purchase that the price bears to earnings.

The calculation can be complicated by the UK system of imputation tax. Companies must pay tax on each distribution of dividends. They are able to offset this tax, however, against mainstream corporation tax, but, for technical reasons it may not be possible to claim it all back. The result is that three price to earnings calculations are possible:

- nil
- net
- max.

The nil calculation assumes there has been no dividend distribution and, therefore, no tax has been paid. The net calculation reduces profit by the amount of unrecoverable tax. The max calculation adds back to profits the maximum tax that could be recovered if all earnings were distributed. Price earnings as reported in the financial press are based on the net system.

This ratio is determined by the market. While the company is very interested in its price to earnings ratio, it has little control over it. Investors give a price to earnings value to a company based on the average level of the market, the industrial sector, the company's products, its management and its financial stability and growth. The company can influence the value a little in the short term by good public relations campaigns. In the long term, however, it must deliver a good return to the equity shareholder to secure a continued high rating.

The advantages of a high price to earnings ratio value are considerable. The wealth of the company's owners is increased in proportion. New funds can be raised at a favourable price, the possibility of a successful hostile takeover bid is much reduced and, finally, the company has the means to make acquisitions on favourable terms by using its 'paper' (shares), as opposed to cash.

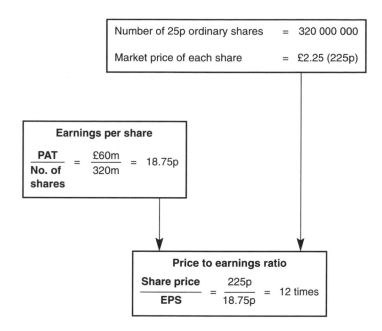

Figure 12.9 Price earnings ratio for the Example Co. PLC

Market to book ratio

The market to book ratio gives the final and, perhaps, the most thorough assessment by the stock market of a company's overall status. It summarises the view of the investing public of the company, its management, its profits, its liquidity, stability and future prospects.

Figure 12.10 shows the calculation. The ratio relates the total market capitalisation of the company to the shareholders' funds. To express it another way, it compares the present stock-market value with the shareholders' investment in the company. The answer will be greater than, less than or equal to unity. Two important questions must be kept in mind when considering this ratio:

- Do the shareholders funds reflect a realistic value for the assets?,
- Is the market rating going through an exceptionally high or low phase?

(Refer to Appendix 1 for various items that can affect this ratio.)

Having got the records of the company into reasonable alignment, the ratio can provide valid information. A value of less than one means that the shareholders' investment has diminished in value; it has wasted away. On the other hand, when this value is well in excess of unity, it means that the investment has been multiplied. It is the investors' perception of the performance of the company in terms of profits, balance sheet strength or liquidity and growth that determines where this ratio will lie.

A high ratio does not simply mean that the worth of the company has increased over time by means of its retained earnings – the multiplier acts in addition to this. Each £1 of original investment, plus each £1 of retained earnings is multiplied by a factor equal to the market to book ratio. To deliver satisfactory performance, management must achieve a market to book ratio of *at least* unity and *preferably* 50 per cent above that.

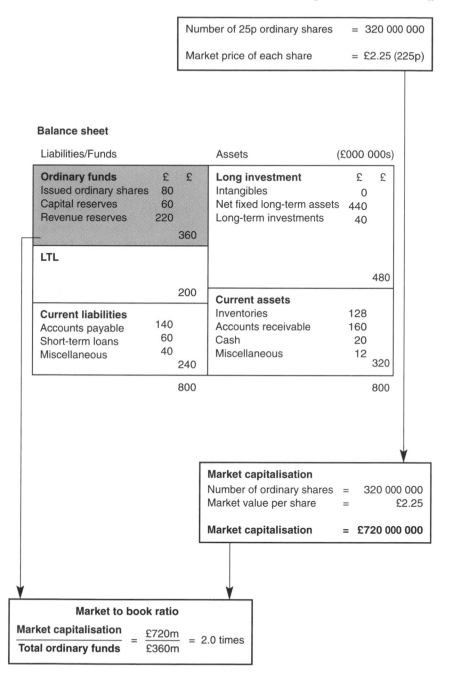

Figure 12.10 Market to book ratio for the Example Co. PLC

Market to book ratio by sector and the FT-SE Companies 1990
This ratio, as with other stock market-related ones, is strongly influenced by
the share price indices at the time. The share prices used in Figure 12.11 are
those of January 1991, when the FT-SE 100 Share Index was just over 2100.

For the FT-SE companies, the published accounts of 1990 were used.
Some companies' accounting periods ended early in the year, others later.
For these later ones, the final profit figures would not have been published,
but sufficient information would have been available for the market to have
made a judgement.

As shown in Figure 12.11 the overall market to book ratio comes out at
almost exactly 2 times. Notwithstanding the relatively low index value at
the time of the sample, this is a high and impressive number. Because 50
per cent of all companies fall *between* 1.3 and 2.8 times, we know that 75
per cent of companies *exceed* that lower limit. It suggests that the value of
1.3 is a *minimum* target for management to aim for. The same chart con-
firms our view that companies falling below 1.0 or 0.9 times are in a most
unsatisfactory state.

Figure 12.11 also shows that three sectors outperform and three under-
perform the market. The two food sectors were obviously favourites with
the investing public at the time. The three sectors of chemicals, stores and
brewing were a little out of favour.

The extraordinarily high rating given to the health sector stands out
starkly once more. This sector has a high operating performance, a good
liquid position and a sustained, high growth rate. With high expectations for
the future, this explains its high price to earnings ratio. These factors combine to produce an outstanding market to book ratio of 4.5 times. (*See*
Appendix 1 – goodwill on acquisition for further comment.)

All

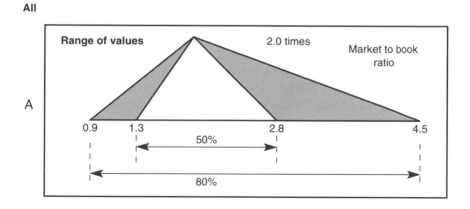

By sectors

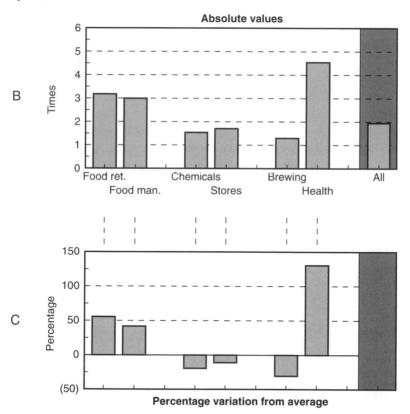

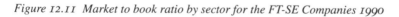

Figure 12.11 Market to book ratio by sector for the FT-SE Companies 1990

13 FINANCIAL LEVERAGE

INTRODUCTION

This chapter brings together material from other chapters to show the relationships between many of the ratios covered so far. Specifically it will:

- establish the financial links between return on total assets and return on equity
- examine further the great importance of the return on equtiy ratio
- link together operating efficiency measures, leverage ratios, valuation factors

so as to identify and quantify all the ratios that drive corporate value. To accomplish this much use will be made of the *V chart* (valuation chart)

FINANCIAL LEVERAGE

The term 'financial engineering' has become quite popular. It is used in relation to schemes for increasing the return to the shareholders from a given return earned by the company. Return on total assets is the measure adopted to measure the overall efficiency of the firm.

The concept of leverage, or, gearing was looked at briefly in Chapter 10, where it was seen that high leverage could substantially increase the return to the shareholder. This chapter will explore further the mechanism of leverage and the links between the return on total assets and return on equity ratios. Figure 13.1 shows these links as:

- debt to equity
- interest
- tax.

The values used in Figure 13.1 are derived from the FT-SE Companies 1990 figures. It will be noted that a pre-tax return on total assets figure of 14 per cent has been converted into an after-tax return on equity figure of 18 per cent. This is leverage in action.

Overleaf, the FT-SE Companies 1990 aggregated accounts are displayed again together with a V chart. This term is used because the chart goes a long way to explain the market valuation of a company.

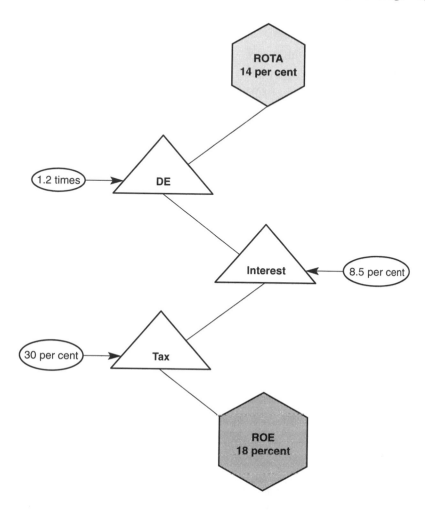

Figure 13.1 The links between return on total assets and return on equity for the FT-SE companies 1990

V CHART

Figure 13.2 illustrates this chart, which looks formidable at first because there seem to be so many parts to it. However, it is worth staying with it because, once the logic is grasped, there is total comprehension of a difficult subject and this whole section becomes very easy to follow.

The chart is constructed on a base that represents the *total funds* in the business. These are divided between *total equity* and *total debt*. At this dividing point, a vertical line, representing return on total assets value (14 per cent in this case) is drawn to scale. At the extreme left there is a vertical line representing the average cost of all debt. It looks low because there is much free debt in the balance sheet (accounts payable and so on). For the FT-SE Companies 1990, 48 per cent of all debt is free and this results in the low average cost of 4.4 per cent.

The upper limits of these two lines are joined by a diagonal line and this is extended to meet a vertical running up from the extreme right of the base. The point where these two lines meet represents the return on equity value (pre-tax). For the FT-SE Companies 1990, the figure is 25.6 per cent. Corporation tax charged in the accounts averages 30 per cent. When we subtract 30 per cent from 25.6 per cent, the answer is the 18 per cent return on equity value.

This explains the whole chart.

Note in particular two values in the chart. **A**, 9.6 per cent, is the difference between the return on total assets figure of 14 per cent and the average interest of 4.4 per cent. **B**, 11.6 per cent is 9.6 per cent multiplied by the debt/equity ratio of 1.2. This latter figure of 11.6 per cent, added to the return on total assets figure of 14 per cent, produces the return on equity value (pre-tax) of 25.6 per cent after tax of 30 per cent. This same figure for return on equity was produced in Chapter 6 using the ratio profit after tax over ordinary funds. What the chart does is identify and quantify the variables that *control* the return on equity ratio. The main piston is return on total assets rising up through the centre and pushing the cantilevered beam upwards. This beam is anchored on the left by the interest rate. Any change in the return on total assets ratio is, therefore, totally reflected on the right-hand column as a change in return on equity (pre-tax), which has a magnification factor derived from the debt/equity ratio.

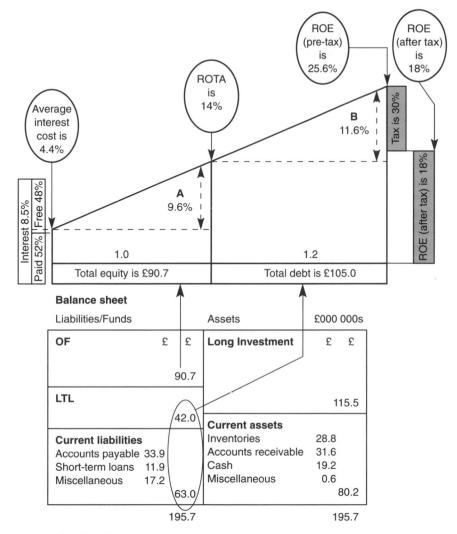

Balance sheet

Liabilities/Funds   Assets   £000 000s

OF	£	£	Long Investment	£	£
		90.7			115.5
LTL					
		42.0	**Current assets**		
Current liabilities			Inventories	28.8	
Accounts payable	33.9		Accounts receivable	31.6	
Short-term loans	11.9		Cash	19.2	
Miscellaneous	17.2		Miscellaneous	0.6	
		63.0			80.2
		195.7			195.7

Profit and loss account

		£
Sales		205.5
PBIT		27.8
	Interest	4.6
PBT		23.2
	Tax	7.0
PAT		16.2
	Dividends	7.3
RE		8.9

Figure 13.2 V chart for the FT-SE Companies 1990

V chart dynamics

The value of 25.6 per cent for return on equity (before tax) can be read directly from the chart in Figure 13.2. It can also be quickly calculated without the chart as there are only three independent inputs:

- return on total assets of 14 per cent
- interest, average cost of, at 4.4 per cent
  - difference (return on total assets less interest), of 9.6 per cent
- debt to equity (times) of 1.2
  - multiply the difference of 9.6 per cent by the debt to equity ratio of 1.2, which is 11.6 per cent
  - add this value to return on total assets
  - result – the return on equity value (pre-tax) of 25.6 per cent.

In one line: ROTA + [(ROTA - Interest) × D/E] = ROE(pre-tax).

Accordingly, using either the chart in Figure 13.2 or the formula above, it is possible to track a change in any one of the input values to its effect on return on equity. (We are still using a return on equity pre-tax value, but, by allowing for tax, we can get through to the return on equity after tax value.)

In Figure 13.3 **A**, the increase of 1 per cent in the return on total assets value, making it 15 per cent, means that application of the formula goes as follows. The 15 per cent value, minus the 4.4 per cent average interest cost, multiplied by the 1.2 times debt/equity ratio, results in a 27.72 per cent return on equity value – an increase of 2.12 per cent on that given for Figure 13.2's parameters.

In **B**, an increase in the debt/equity ratio to 1.75 has the following result when the formula is applied. The 14 per cent return on total assets value, minus the 4.4 per cent average interest cost, multiplied by the increased 1.75 times debt/equity ratio, results in a 16.8 per cent return on equity value – an increase of 5.2 per cent on that given for Figure 13.2's parameters.

In **C**, an increase in the interest cost of 0.6 per cent to 5 per cent alters things as follows. The 14 per cent return on total assets value, minus the 5 per cent average interest cost, multiplied by the 1.2 debt/equity ratio, results in a 24.8 per cent return on equity value – a decrease of 0.8 per cent on that given for Figure 13.2's parameters.

The effects of the variables that link the return on total assets and return on equity ratios have been fully quantified by this process of analysis. It only remains to link return on equity to company corporate value to complete the linkage from stock-market value to shop-floor variables. This will be addressed overleaf.

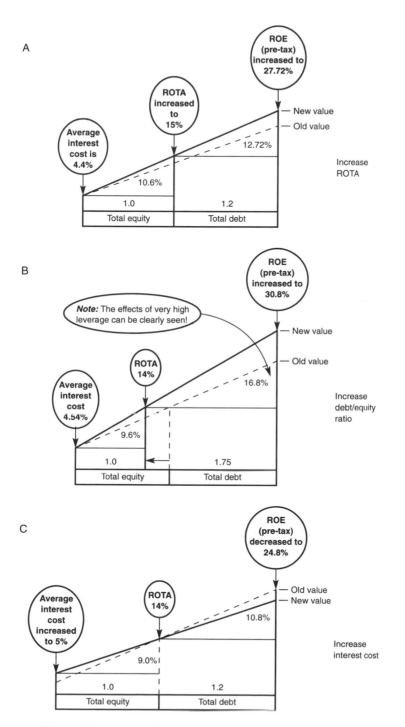

Figure 13.3 Effects of changes in values on V chart

MARKET TO BOOK RATIO

In Figure 13.4, you will see the balance sheet, profit and loss account, share data and important ratios that we have accumulated so far for the Example Co. PLC.

The new element is the box below the ratios headed Total Company, Single Share and Internal return v required return. In the columns below these headings, three further relationships are developed, each of which results in the same answer – 2 times. This is the *market to book ratio* for the Example Co. PLC. An understanding of the messages being delivered by these calculations is important.

A Total company

Under the heading *total company* is the standard market to book ratio calculation. This gives us the relationship between the value as determined by the investing community and the value of the shareholders' investment in the books of the company. A value of less than one is an indictment of management's performance because the company is being sold at a marked down price, like sub-standard goods in a sale. Good companies, on the other hand, produce values of 1.5 and upwards.

B Single share

Single share is simply the market to book ratio as it applies to one, single share. The total number of ordinary shares is divided into market capitalisation (above the line) and ordinary funds (below the line) to give the ratio share price to book value.

C Internal return v required return

This is an important ratio that we have not met before. It relates the return on equity of the company to the earnings yield (K) on the share. It is a relationship that has important consequences for management and it will be dealt with next.

| Number of 25p ordinary shares | = | 320 000 000 |
| Market price of each share | = | £2.25 (225p) |

Profit and loss account

Balance sheet

	£
Sales	1120
Operating costs	1008
PBIT	112
Interest	20
PBT	92
Tax	32
PAT	60
Dividends	24
RE	36

Liabilities/Funds   Assets   (£000 000s)

Ordinary funds	£	£	**FA**	£	£
Issued ordinary shares	80				
Capital reserves	60				
Revenue reserves	220				
		360			
LTL					480
		200	**CA**		
CL					
		240			320
		800			800

Important ratios

Book value per share	Total ordinary funds./No. of shares	= £360/320	= 112.5p
Market capitalisation	No. of shares × Market price	= 320×225p	= £720
Return on equity (ROE)	PAT/OF × 100	= £60/£360 × 100	= 16.6%
Earnings yield ('K')	EPS/Share price × 100	= 18.7p/225p × 100	= 8.3%

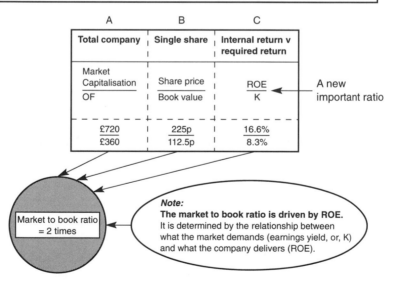

	A	**B**	**C**
	Total company	Single share	Internal return v required return
	$\dfrac{\text{Market Capitalisation}}{\text{OF}}$	$\dfrac{\text{Share price}}{\text{Book value}}$	$\dfrac{\text{ROE}}{\text{K}}$ ← A new important ratio
	£720 / £360	225p / 112.5p	16.6% / 8.3%

Market to book ratio = 2 times

Note:
The market to book ratio is driven by ROE. It is determined by the relationship between what the market demands (earnings yield, or, K) and what the company delivers (ROE).

Figure 13.4 Further developments on the market to book ratio applied to data from he Example Co. Ltd

THE IMPORTANCE OF THE RETURN ON EQUITY RATIO

In Figure 13.5 we continue to examine the relationship between return on equity and 'K'. We can go back to Chapter 12 to take a second look at this. 'K' is a shorthand way of expressing the earnings yield. This value is calculated by taking earnings per share and dividing by the market price of the share. It expresses the rate of return earned by the investor who buys at today's price. (To get at the *true* return to the investor, we need take account of growth in the earnings per share values, but we shall ignore this for the purposes of this illustration.)

This 'K' moves inversely with the share price: when the share price rises, the yield decreases and vice versa. The yield is, therefore, determined by the market place. If sentiment goes against the company, investors sell shares, the price per share falls and the 'K' increases until a new equilibrium is reached where the higher yield compensates shareholders for the less attractive share. If a company has high-yielding shares, it implies that the company is not favoured by investors. The 'K' is the rate of return demanded by the investing public to stay with the company.

Return on equity is the rate of return being provided by the company to these same investors. Any difference between return on equity value and 'K' is reflected in the company being valued at a premium or discount. If return on equity is 12 per cent and 'K' is 8 per cent the company will be marked up in price to a 50 per cent premium.

The 'K' value is, therefore, a target set by the market place for management achievement. Return on equity should not, in normal conditions, fall below 'K'. In most companies, it should be a certain multiple of 'K', for example, 1.5 to 2.5 times. Of course, yield values change with every movement in the Stock Exchange's indices, but one must pick some 'normal' level as a base target.

The important conclusion is that, from any particular 'K' position, return on equity drives both company *and* shareholder value.

The market to book ratio is a reflection of the internal rate of return being delivered by the company to the shareholder with the rate of return demanded externally by the market.
Below are the main factors that influence both these variables.

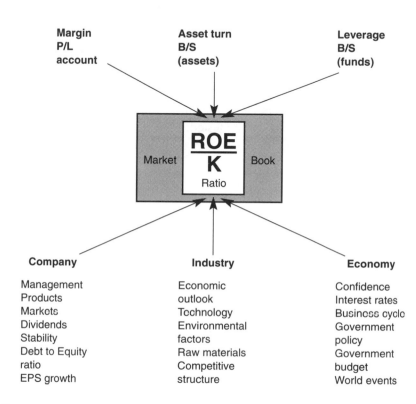

Margin   **Asset turn**   **Leverage**
P/L   B/S   B/S
account   (assets)   (funds)

Market $$\frac{ROE}{K}$$ Book
Ratio

Company   **Industry**   **Economy**

Management   Economic   Confidence
Products   outlook   Interest rates
Markets   Technology   Business cycle
Dividends   Environmental   Government
Stability   factors   policy
Debt to Equity   Raw materials   Government
ratio   Competitive   budget
EPS growth   structure   World events

Figure 13.5 The importance of the return on equity ratio and earnings yield (K) relationship

CORPORATE VALUE

In Figure 13.6 we are now able to pull together the various sections of the overall corporate valuation model. **A** in the figure repeats the operating perfomance model given in Chapter 7. **B** shows the financial gearing model given earlier in this chapter. **C** brings in the stock-market ratios covered in Chapter 12. This completes the chain that links shop floor value drivers to the stock market value. Figures from the FT-SE Companies 1990 accounts are used for the various nodes in the model. There is an arithmetical link from every variable in the system right up to final corporate value of £181.4bn.

The impact of a 1 per cent improvement in sales margin brought about by a small decrease in costs can be tested. It would yield a new return on total assets of 15.3 per cent (there is some small degree of rounding because only one decimal place is used). From the V chart we can read off that a return on total assets of 15.3 per cent would translate into a return on equity (after tax) of 19.8 per cent. Using the equation return on equity over 'K', a return on equity of 19.8 per cent with a 'K' of 9 per cent would give a market to book ratio of 2.2 times. This ratio applied to the ordinary funds figure of £90.7bn produces a total market value of just under £200bn against the current value of £181.4bn.

The total number of independent variables in the model that can be influenced by management can now be identified:

- the cost percentages in the profit and loss account, principally: material, labour and overheads
- the main asset groups in the balance sheet, namely: fixed assets, inventories and accounts receivable
- debt to equity ratio
- interest
- tax

An increase in the debt/equity value has a double effect, it increases return on equity but it also increases risk and therefore normally results in a higher 'K' value. The increase in return on equity should increase corporate value but if debt/equity is pushed beyond a prudent level the resulting increase in 'K' will actually reduce total value.

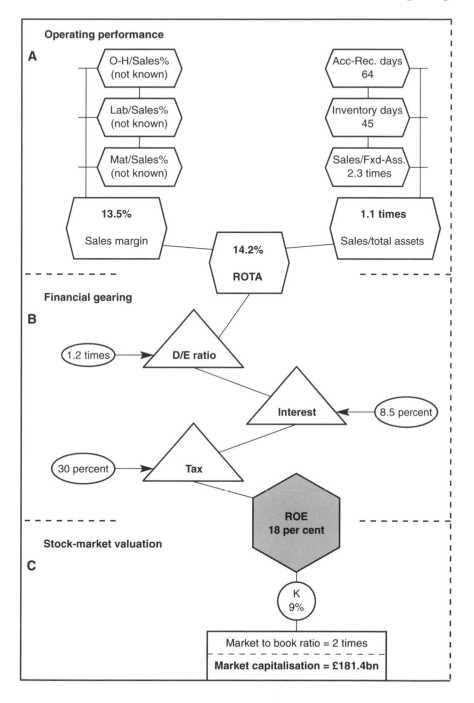

Figure 13.6 Overall corporate valuation model for the FT-SE Companies 1990

14 SUSTAINABLE GROWTH

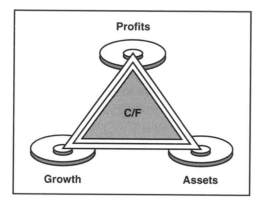

Figure 14.1 Growth and the need for balance

GROWTH

Growth is to a company like medicine is to a patient – beneficial up to a certain level, but dangerous and possibly fatal when that level is exceeded. There is a need for balance (*see* Figure 14.1). Given the opportunities and corresponding dangers of growth, particularly in times of high inflation, it is wise to consider whether there is some way in which we can specify for a company what level of growth it can safely absorb.

This chapter illustrates one particular method that has been found useful. To assist in our analysis, we will take the case of the CABCO Construction Company shown in Figure 14.2. This is a company that is suffering from severe problems of growth. The figures have been disguised but not exaggerated. The calendar years and, of course, the name of the company have been changed.

We see a company that has been growing, in terms of sales, at approximately 15 per cent per annum. However, it has a rapidly deteriorating financial position, as measured by the current ratio, that has dropped from 2.3 to 1.4 times over the four years and the debt to total assets ratio has risen from 37 per cent to 61 per cent over the same period. The liquidity ratios were very strong in 1985 but have sunk to their lowest acceptable level by 1989. The most worrying aspect of the figures is the speed at which the liquidity position has deteriorated.

Performance, as measured by return on equity, was low but improved significantly in 1989. It made a passable return of almost 20 per cent before tax to its shareholders, but it is now close to a liquidity crisis. Accordingly, management must take urgent action to stop the downward trend and change the direction in which the company is going.

This chapter is concerned with the problem of identifying and quantifying the options open to management, but, more importantly, it will extract general rules relating to company growth and how it should be handled.

Balance sheets	1985 £	1987 £	1989 £
OF	661	654	696
CL	388	584	1096
Total	1049	1238	1792
FA	159	272	271
CA	890	966	1521
Total	1049	1238	1792

Income statistics

Sales	1325	1766	2280
PBIT	85	56	184
Tax	41	14	67
Dividends	23	19	23
RE	18	3	44

Ratios

Current ratio (times)	2.3 times	1.6 times	1.4 times
Debt to Total assets (%)	37%	47%	61%
ROE (pre-tax)	13%	6%	20%
Share price	90p	70p	110p
Number of shares	320	320	320

Note: Fall in liquidity ratios

Note: Average growth rate over 4 years = 15 per cent

Figure 14.2 Growth example: CABCO Construction Ltd – summary accounts for years 1985, 1987 and 1989

IDENTIFYING PROBLEMS

The CABCO balance sheet for 1985 and 1989 are shown roughly to scale in Figure 14.3. The size of the 1989 balance sheet is 70 per cent greater than that for 1985. When we look at the changes in the different balance sheet boxes the major expansion is in both current assets and current liabilities. An explosion in size of the former has been financed almost entirely by the latter. The company has drifted from a strong base into an unstable, high-risk position and, if the drift continues, bankruptcy is the likely result – or at least a change of ownership and control.

The immediate problem is an excess of short-term borrowings. Most definitely, these must *not* be increased and, if possible, they should be reduced. Possible courses of action to which management has already given consideration are:

- reducing investment in current assets, either absolutely or at least as a proportion of sales
- introducing long-term funds in the form of loans or equity.

Because of industry custom, the situation and history of the business, management were of the opinion that current assets could not be reduced relative to sales, so attention was, therefore, concentrated on the possibility of finding additional long-term funds. The questions they had to answer were:

- 'How much?'
- 'What form – equity or loan?'
- 'If loan, what term of years?'

When cash flow forecasts were produced, it quickly became evident that a long-term loan would not solve the problem as such borrowed money could not be repaid. Instead, more and more borrowings would be required because of the negative cash flow that this company generated each year. By *negative* cash flow is meant that sufficient funds are not being generated, which, together with normal borrowings, will fund the assets required by the operations.

Companies in this negative cash flow position have a form of financial diabetes, that is, they have a perpetual cash haemorrhage because of the values of certain operating parameters. It is necessary to identify and quantify the factors behind this condition.

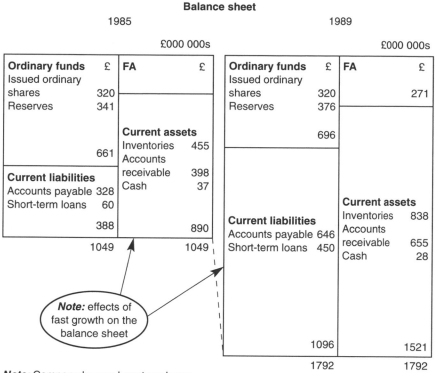

Note: Company has no long-term loans

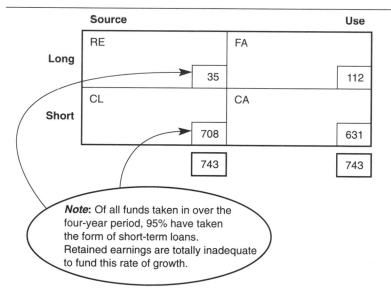

Figure 14.3 Movement in CABCO Construction Ltd's accounts over four years drawn roughly to scale

ANALYSIS

Figure 14.4 extracts some of the basic figures for 1989. The following are the critical values:

- sales   £2280
- current assets of   £1521
- retained earnings of £   44

It will be shown that it is the interrelationships between these three values, combined with the rate of growth experienced by the company, that has given rise to its present financing problem. These three values, with a growth rate of 15 per cent collectively, give rise to a strong negative cash flow.

The relationship of current assets to sales is £0.67 – each £1 of sales requires 67p to carry it. For every increase of £1000 sales next year, £670 of extra current assets will be needed. This will require £670 of extra funds in the balance sheet.

The relationship of retained earnings to sales is £0.02 – each £1 of sales generates 2p of retained earnings which goes into balance sheet funds. Each £1 of existing sales generates 2p funds, but remember each extra £1 sales requires 67p. *Therefore £33 of existing sales this year are needed to fund £1 of extra sales next year.* This ratio of £1 extra sales on £33 existing gives a growth rate of 3 per cent. This rate of 3 per cent is the rate of growth in current assets the company can fund from its retained earnings, but the company has been growing at *15 per cent* over the last 4 years. The excess growth of 12 per cent has been funded by borrowing. In this company, all the borrowing has been short term, hence the financing problem.

Current sales are £2280. If 12 per cent of this has to be funded *externally* next year at the rate of 67p for each £1 sales, the company will have to borrow an extra £180. The following year it will need to borrow £180, increased by 15 per cent and so on, indefinitely. This imbalance between the variables is explored next.

Balance sheet

1989

£000's

Ordinary funds	£	Fixed assets	£
Issued ordinary shares	320		271
Capital reserves	376		
	696		

£000's
Extract from income statement
Sales £2280

Retained earnings £44

		Current assets	
Current liabilities		Inventories	838
Accounts payable	646	Accounts	
Short-term loans	450	receivable	655
		Cash	28
	1096		1521
	1792		1792

Critical relationships

Current assets to sales $\dfrac{£1521}{£2280}$ = **£0.67**

Retained earnings to sales $\dfrac{£44}{£2280}$ = **£0.02**

Growth in sales – historic rate 1985-89 $\left[\left\{\dfrac{£2280}{£1325}\right\}^{\frac{1}{4}} - 1\right] \times 100 = \textbf{15\%}$

Note: It takes a few moments to realise that the relationship between these two values is 3% and that this is the growth rate in current assets that can be funded directly from retained earnings.

Actual growth is 15%, therefore only a fifth of growth has been funded from the internal resources. The remaining 12% has been funded by borrowed money.

Figure 14.4 Critical asset, profit and growth relationships in CABCO Construction Ltd's accounts

GROWTH EQUILIBRIUM

The *growth equilibrium* equation is given in Figure 14.5. It takes the values resulting from the three critcal relationships shown in Figure 14.4 (defined using the symbols T, R and G) (Section A). It puts these values together to derive a cash flow position – E. When E = 1, cash flow is neutral; values greater than 1 show a positive cash flow and vice versa. The values for CABCO give a result of one fifth, (Section B) which is the portion of the growth that is self-funded. Many readers will have valid questions at this stage about some underlying assumptions in the model. However, this is an early and primitive, but useful, version of a more generalised growth model that will be developed later in the chapter.

This version relies on the relationship between current assets and retained earnings. It is valid for a company in the situation of CABCO Construction Company that is heavily current assets based and heavily borrowed. The version is also useful, with slight amendments, for trading companies and rapidly growing small businesses, with or without high inflation problems. It integrates cash flow with the following three ratios:

- current assets to sales
- retained earnings to sales
- growth in sales.

These three powerful cash flow drivers having been identified, management's attention can be focused on the essentials. In Figure 14.5 (Section C), three single-value options are worked out to highlight an approach to the problem. It is not likely that any one of these in isolation could be successful, but the combination strategy at the end (or some other variation of all three) could provide a satisfactory solution.

The message from the growth equilibrium model is that the flow of cash results from other variables in the operation of the company. If the values are such that this flow is heavily negative, then either the variables have to be changed or plans need to be made to fund the negative cash flow. This funding need must be identified *well before* it happens and the necessary resources secured before the situation becomes critical. If it is left too late, then the company will be impossible to fund.

Growth
equilibrium

$$\frac{R}{G \times T} = E$$

A

Symbols	Critical relationships	Values expressed decimally
T	Current assets to sales	0.67
R	Retained earnings to sales	0.02
G	Growth in sales	0.15

B

$$\frac{R}{G \times T} = E \qquad \frac{0.02}{0.15 \times 0.67} = \frac{1}{5}$$

Existing position and strategy 1
The one-fifth fraction shows the part of the existing growth that is being funded by retained earnings. There is a cash deficit for the remainder. The value of this expression must be brought up to unity to achieve a neutral cash flow. Three options are shown below.

C

$$\frac{R}{G \times T} = E \qquad \frac{0.02}{0.03 \times 0.67} = \frac{1}{1}$$

Option 1
Reduce growth to 3 per cent.

- -

$$\frac{R}{G \times T} = E \qquad \frac{0.10}{0.15 \times 0.67} = \frac{1}{1}$$

Option 2
Increase retentions to 10 per cent.

- -

$$\frac{R}{G \times T} = E \qquad \frac{0.02}{0.15 \times 0.135} = \frac{1}{1}$$

Option 3
Reduce assets to sales ratio to 13.5 per cent.

$$\frac{R}{G \times T} = E \qquad \frac{0.05}{0.10 \times 0.50} = \frac{1}{1}$$

Combination strategy
- increase retentions to 5 per cent
- reduce growth to 10 per cent
- reduce assets to sales ratio to 50 per cent.

Any of these four will wipe out the cash deficit:

Figure 14.5 Growth equilibrium calculations for CABCO Construction Ltd

General model of growth equilibrium

The equation used in Figure 14.5 suited that particular limited situation because the company was a low user of fixed assets and it was also very highly borrowed. The limitations of the equation were that:

• it looked only at current rather than total assets
• it ignored the ability of most companies to supplement retained earnings with funds from other sources.

Figure 14.6 illustrates the changes that are required in order to make the formula more generally applicable. (It is not necessary to emphasise that a company should not be run only according to formulae. What formulae can do, however, is provide a shorthand approach to identifying problems that might arise. These can then be examined in depth, taking into account the particular conditions in the company.)

The first change is to include all the assets in the balance sheet that will be affected by growth. The second is to allow for balanced funding, that is both loans *and* equity. For each £1 of retained earnings, how much borrowing is prudent? The desired debt/equity ratio of the company will provide the answer to this question. Each £1 of retained earnings will support at least £1 and perhaps £1.50 in borrowings.

If the exercise takes in all the assets and if it accepts the existing mix of funds in the balance sheet, then what is left is the top left-hand box. Ordinary funds is the only section of the balance sheet that has to be funded by retained earnings. Accordingly, a good rule of thumb for a self-funding growth formula is to relate retained earnings to owners' funds.

The assumptions in this formula are important. They are that growth in sales will be matched exactly by growth in current assets and fixed assets. It is further assumed that profits, interest, tax and dividends will grow likewise. Finally, it is assumed that a constant debt to equity ratio will apply. If these conditions are met, then Figure 14.6 tells us that the self-funding rate of growth for a company can be calculated by expressing the retained earnings as a percentage of owners' funds (using the opening balance sheet for the period). Growth in excess of this rate will require extra equity or will cause a weakening in ratios.

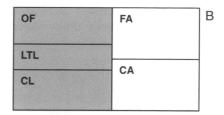

OF	FA
LTL	CA
CL	

Original growth formula A
It considered the funding of CA only.
It did not allow for funds in excess of RE
as being available for financing of growth.

Change 1:
Growth in the short term may affect only
CA, but, in the long term, increases in
FA must also be funded.

OF	FA	B
LTL	CA	
CL		

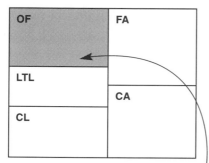

OF	FA
LTL	CA
CL	

Change 2: C
The normal, healthy company can rely
on borrowing to supplement RE. The
relationship between RE and extra
borrowings can be ascertained from
the existing or desired D/E ratio.

Note: We have therefore moved from the bottom right-hand corner
of the B/S to the top left-hand one. In the original formula the CA to
sales ratio was examined. It is more generally applicable, however,
if the OF to sales ratio is used as the T variable.

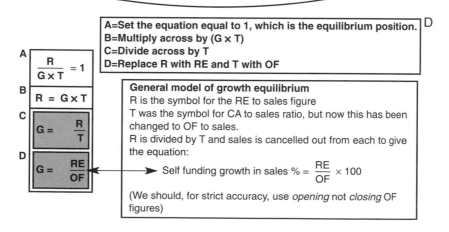

A=Set the equation equal to 1, which is the equilibrium position. D
B=Multiply across by (G × T)
C=Divide across by T
D=Replace R with RE and T with OF

A $$\frac{R}{G \times T} = 1$$

B $$R = G \times T$$

C $$G = \frac{R}{T}$$

D $$G = \frac{RE}{OF}$$

General model of growth equilibrium
R is the symbol for the RE to sales figure
T was the symbol for CA to sales ratio, but now this has been
changed to OF to sales.
R is divided by T and sales is cancelled out from each to give
the equation:

Self funding growth in sales % = $\frac{RE}{OF} \times 100$

(We should, for strict accuracy, use *opening* not *closing* OF
figures)

Figure 14.6 General model for growth equilibrium calculations

Self-funding growth and the FT-SE Companies 1990
As Figure 14.7 shows, the general model of the growth equilibrium equation in Figure 14.6 produces a value of 12 per cent average for the FT-SE Companies 1990, with 50 per cent of the sample lying between 9 per cent and 20 per cent. These numbers are quite high. With inflation as low as 3 to 4 per cent it suggests that they have the capacity to expand in real terms at 8 per cent (extraordinary items are excluded from retained earnings in these calculations).

  Given that the developed economies, in stable times in the long term, grow at 4 per cent maximum, these companies are significantly outgrowing the economy. One can see why so many of them are involved in takeover bids.
In the sectors chart, the extraordinarily high potential of the health companies can be seen. It is in excess of 20 per cent. This sector is followed by the two food sectors – both of which have self-funding growth rates in excess of 15 per cent. The chemical and brewing sectors include very heavy asset-type companies. In such companies, growth soaks up a great deal of funds, so high growth rates are difficult to fund.

APPLICATION TO ACQUISITIONS
Many groups acquire fast-growing businesses to sustain the growth of the parent. The post acquisition positive or negative cash flow from such acquisitions is of crucial importance. A company with heavy asset requirements, whether these are fixed or current assets, that grows rapidly, will need lots of funds to keep its balance sheet ratios in sound condition. If the company is very profitable, these funds may be generated internally. However, if it has only medium or low profits, then funds will have to be provided by the parent company. The total cost of such a company over a number of years could be many times its original purchase price.

  The most valuable business to own or buy is one with high growth and high profits. The least valuable one is not a low growth, low profit company. Such a company is not worth very much, but it is not dangerous. The worst company is one with high growth and low profits. If such a company also has a high asset to sales ratio, then it has, within itself, all the makings of a financial disaster.

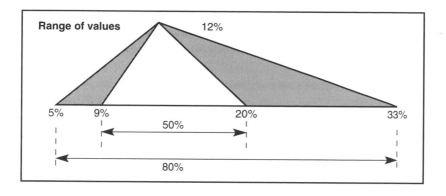

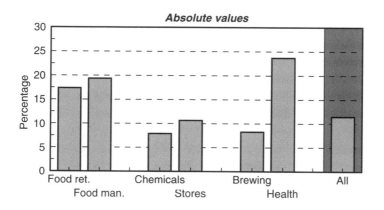

Figure 14.7 Self-funding growth rate for the FT-SE Companies 1990 (excluding extra-ordinary items)

Part V

MANAGEMENT DECISION MAKING

15 COST, VOLUME AND PRICE

COST, VOLUME AND PRICE RELATIONSHIPS

The internal operating dynamics of the business are more often than not quite complicated and not ideal: more sales do not necessarily mean more profits, the price we would like to sell for is generally ten per cent above what our competitors are charging or the manager is constantly being asked to get costs down or to sell at or below the total cost figure.

How is it possible to make profits in this scenario? There is no magic answer, but, what we can do is to recognise that the main function of cost accounting is to identify the areas where profit is possible. This means understanding how costs behave – in particular, how they respond to changes in the variables: price, volume and, above all, product mix. It was mentioned earlier that the performance model which copes well with the big business scene is not good at this level of detail. However, it is at this level that profits are made and lost. Also, it is at this level that day-to-day decisions are made as to what price to quote for a job, whether to accept or reject a price on offer, whether and how to pay commission to salespeople and so on.

The monthly management accounts supplied to managers are often used by them as information on which to base their decision making. However, the way in which the information is presented is often not helpful for this purpose. For instance, costs may be classified in a way that does not allow their recalculation on the basis of an alternative course of action.

This chapter will illustrate a series of calculations around this subject that enable managers to tread their way through the difficulties in safety. These are essential, interesting and powerful tools. In the following pages we will work through a number of examples that show their application.

COSTING ILLUSTRATION

Figure 15.1 shows a budget for the company Lawnmowers Ltd. We will use the numbers to illustrate some fundamental facts about the behaviour of costs. These numbers are kept very simple and fundamental so that they will embed themselves in the mind very quickly. We will then do many calculations around them. The crucial facts are:

- this company has only one product, which it sells for a unit price of £200
- it plans to manufacture and sell 1000 units in the coming year at a profit of £20 each
- the total cost of £180 consists of the elements shown in Figure 15.1.

The company has received an offer from a very large retailer to purchase 200 extra units at the special price of £160. The Sales Manager is faced with the dilemma of whether the company can sell at a price that is below the calculated total cost and still bring benefit to the company. (The marketing implications of selling at a special, low price are, of course, very significant, but, for this exercise, they will be ignored in order to tease out the financial aspects.)

We instinctively know that the total cost as shown in the budget will change if the forecast number of units is changed. The manager could, therefore, recalculate the total cost per unit after allowing for the extra volume of 200. This would give a revised overall profit.

The decision could be made on the basis of this type of calculation, but it would not help much in determining the lowest price that could be charged in a really competitive situation. Neither would it be of very much use for producing a whole set of scenarios for sales of different volumes at different prices.

An alternative approach is illustrated in the following pages.

	No. of Units	Per Unit	Totals
Sales	1000	£200	£200 000
Direct costs			
Materials	1000	£75	£75 000
Labour	1000	£45	£45 000
	1000	£120	£120 000
Overhead costs			
Administration		£40	£40 000
Selling		£20	£20 000
Total cost		£180	£180 000
Profit		£20	£20 000
		£200	£200 000

Note: Total cost is £180, but can the firm sell at £160 *and* make a profit ?

Figure 15.1 Summary budget for Lawnmowers Ltd

Cost classification

Of the many ways in which costs can be classified, possibly the most useful for decision making purposes is on the basis of their response to volume changes. This well-known classification uses the following terms:

- *Fixed costs* These are costs where the total expenditure does not change with the level of activity. For instance rent of a factory will not increase or decrease if volume of throughput goes up or down by 10 per cent.
- *Variable costs* These vary directly with changes in output. The cost of materials consumed in the product will vary almost in direct proportion to changes in volume. An interesting paradox is that a fully variable cost is always a fixed charge per unit irrespective of volume. On the other hand, fixed costs charged to each unit fall with volume increases.

In practice, there are very few, if any, costs that are either totally fixed or totally variable across the whole range of possible outputs from a plant. However, it is useful for our example to make some simplifying assumptions. The fixed and variable costs for Lawnmowers Ltd are shown in Figure 15.2.

The variable costs are:

- material
- labour.

In practice, while direct materials are almost always fully variable, direct labour is more likely to be at least partially fixed.

The fixed costs are:

- administration
- selling costs.

This assumption implies that these amounts will not change at all with any forecast changes in volume.

The variable and fixed costs per unit – £120 and £60 respectively – add to a total cost of £180. Note from earlier that management is faced with the question of whether or not to accept a large order at a price of £160 per unit.

	No. of Units	Per Unit	Totals
Sales	1000	£200	£200 000
Direct costs			
Materials	1000	£75	£75 000
Labour	1000	£45	£45 000
	1000	£120	£120 000
Overhead costs			
Administration		£40	£40 000
Selling		£20	£20 000
Total cost		£180	£180 000
Profit		£20	£20 000
		£200	£200 000

Cost classifications

Fixed costs: totals not affected by volume.

Variable costs: totals vary directly with volume.

Figure 15.2 Fixed and variable costs for Lawnmowers Ltd

Contribution

The division of costs into fixed and variable allows us to re-examine unit costs. Figure 15.3 shows two different layouts:

- traditional cost approach
- contribution approach.

In the traditional breakdown the unit selling price of £200 is split into:

- variable cost of £120
- fixed cost £60
- profit £20.

With the contribution approach, however, the selling price is split into two sections only:

- variable cost of £120
- contribution of £80.

Contribution, therefore, replaces the figures of fixed cost of £60 and profit of £20. This figure of contribution is an important and useful concept. It is therefore worthwhile spending some time examining it.

Cash flow and contribution

We have arrived at the contribution figure of £80 by adding back the fixed cost of £60 to the profit of £20. However, we can see that it is also the result of deducting variable cost from the selling price. This latter definition is the most useful one and we will extract cash flow meaning from it. Each extra unit sold at the budget price of £200 creates a cash in-flow of that amount. However, this same unit increases variable costs by £120. These are direct cash costs and there will be a corresponding cash out-flow. *One extra unit sold gives rise to extra revenue of £200 and extra cash costs of £120. The difference of £80, which we call contribution, is the net cash in-flow resulting from an extra unit sold.*

The £80 cash sacrificed from the loss of one unit is even more obvious. The company loses £200 revenue but saves only £120 costs. There will be no saving of fixed costs, so the cash loss, again, is £80. Contribution can therefore be defined as the *net cash flow from a single transaction.* In other words, it is the cash gained from the sale of an extra unit or the cash lost from the sale of one less unit.

The relationship that contribution has to profit will be pursued in the following pages.

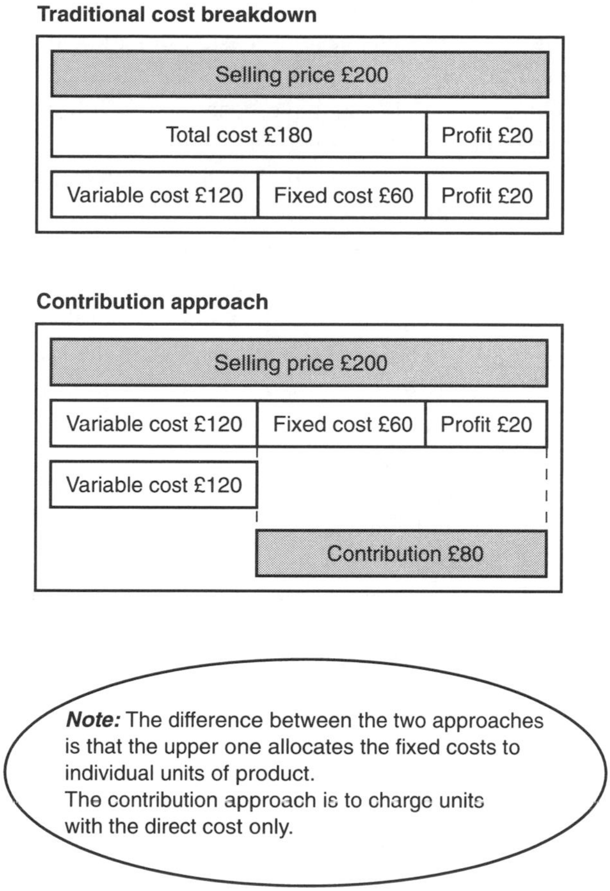

Traditional cost breakdown

Selling price £200		
Total cost £180		Profit £20
Variable cost £120	Fixed cost £60	Profit £20

Contribution approach

Selling price £200		
Variable cost £120	Fixed cost £60	Profit £20
Variable cost £120		
	Contribution £80	

Note: The difference between the two approaches is that the upper one allocates the fixed costs to individual units of product.
The contribution approach is to charge units with the direct cost only.

Figure 15.3 Alternative costing approaches applied to Lawnmowers Ltd's figures

Contribution and profit
Contribution flows into the business as cash from the sale of each unit. However, it is not free cash because it must first be allocated to the payment of fixed costs. Once the fixed costs have been paid in full, the contribution stream goes straight into profit.

Figure 15.4 illustrates the process. It shows two water tanks to represent volumes of fixed costs and profit respectively. The fixed cost tank has a capacity of £60 000. Each unit sold pumps £80 into this tank. When a sufficient number of £80s have filled this tank with cash, then all the extra contribution overflows into the profit tank. It is easy to see that the cash from the first 750 units (750 × £80 = £60 000) *remains* in the fixed cost tank; it is only the cash from units *in excess of 750* that goes to profit. If the company sells its budgeted volume of 1000 units, then the final 250 units will provide profits of £20 000 (250 × £80). This important figure of £80 is referred to as *contribution per unit (CPU)*. It is used a great deal in contribution analysis and you will come across it many times.

Looking back at the original budget statement, it is possible to see that it is not fully correct to say that the profit of £20 000 is earned as a profit of £20 on *each* of the 1000 units; it is more realistic to say that *no profit at all* is made on the first 750 units, but *from that point onwards*, £80 profit per unit is achieved.

Figure 15.4 also highlights a second important concept, which is *total contribution*. The total contribution in this plant is £80 000. In the upper part of the diagram it is shown as **units multiplied by CPU**. In the lower part, the same figure is produced from **fixed costs plus profit**. We will find ourselves making use of this formula in many situations.

A fundamental principle underlying the logic of this chapter is that our objective is to '**maximise contribution**'. In following this principle the greatest profit can be achieved.

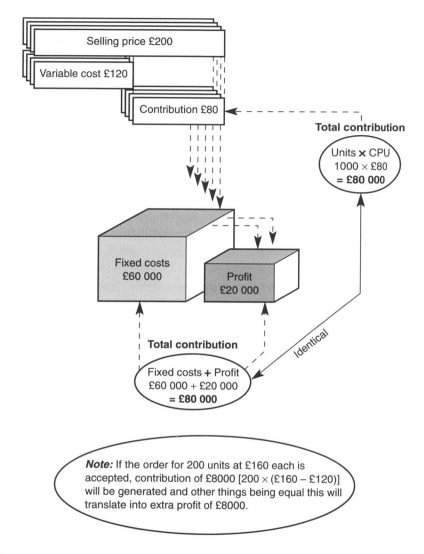

Selling price £200

Variable cost £120

Contribution £80

Total contribution

Units × CPU
1000 × £80
= £80 000

Fixed costs
£60 000

Profit
£20 000

Total contribution

Fixed costs **+** Profit
£60 000 + £20 000
= £80 000

Identical

Note: If the order for 200 units at £160 each is accepted, contribution of £8000 [200 × (£160 − £120)] will be generated and other things being equal this will translate into extra profit of £8000.

Figure 15.4 Contribution's relationship to fixed costs and profit

Total contribution

The two ways just mentioned in which to look at total contribution are expressed in an important equation in Figure 15.5:

- units × CPU = fixed cost + profit.

This view of the cost dynamics of the company facilitates many interesting calculations we can do with volume, cost and profits. For instance, we can start at 'units' and ascertain without difficulty what the profit would be at any level of unit sales. Alternatively we can work from the profit side and ask what unit sales are needed to deliver any desired level of profit. Finally we can combine price and volume changes and instantly translate them into profit.

For instance:

1) What profit would result from an increase in sales of 10%?

Answer £28,000

2) How many units must be sold to provide a profit of £32,000?

Answer 1150 units

3) Finally, a very important question, how many units must be sold to break even, i.e. make neither a profit nor a loss

Answer 750 units

This latter calculation gives the *break-even point*. The concept of break-even is one that is used widely in business. The formula for its calculation in terms of units is derived directly from the above equation. We simply set profit equal to zero and solve for the number of units. We will look at this concept some more in the following pages.

It is important to remember that we are still thinking in terms of *physical* units. The formulae and methods illustrated above work only in the case of a business that sells one type of unit. However, this limited formula provides a useful stepping off point for the next stage. As soon as the fundamentals have been grasped, it is possible to move easily to the more general case where we can do calculations for a company that produces many different units.

Basic equation

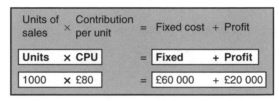

Units of sales	×	Contribution per unit	=	Fixed cost	+ Profit
Units	×	CPU	=	Fixed	+ Profit
1000	×	£80	=	£60 000	+ £20 000

1 | **Effect of increase in sales**

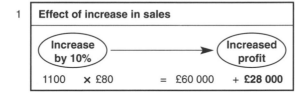

1100 × £80 = £60 000 + **£28 000**

2 | **Number of units to provide required profit**

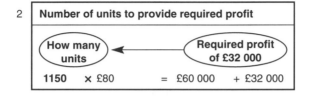

1150 × £80 = £60 000 + £32 000

3 | **Number of units that must be sold to break even – the break-even calculation**

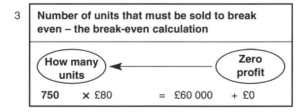

750 × £80 = £60 000 + £0

Figure 15.5 Total contribution – the important relationship between contribution per unit and fixed costs and profit – for Lawnmowers Ltd

Break even (B/E)

The importance of the break-even level of output has been mentioned. It is the level at which the company makes neither a loss nor a profit, just covers its fixed costs. It is, therefore, a most important cross-over point in a plant's level of activity and so managers pay much attention to it.

The break even chart is a well-known illustration of the concept. It shows the relationship over the total range of output between the three important components:

- fixed costs
- variable costs
- revenue.

The *horizontal axis* in Figure 15.6 is used to represent *activity*, which can be expressed in different ways, such as percentage of capacity, machine hours and so on. For our purposes here, both the number of units produced and capacity percentage are used. The full range – from zero output to the full plant capacity of 1500 units – is shown.

The *vertical axis* is used to plot costs and revenue. Figures from Lawn-mowers Ltd are used for each of the three components (fixed costs, variable costs and revenue.) These are plotted in three separate charts in Figure 15.6.

Chart A illustrates the fixed costs, represented by a horizontal line at the £60,000 point on the vertical axis. This line is absolutely horizontal because fixed costs do not go up or down with changes in the level of output.

Chart B illustrates the variable costs: At zero output there are no variable costs, but, with each unit sold, the total grows by £120. At 600 units variable costs amount to £72,000. The relationship with output is strictly linear, hence the straight line sloping upwards.

Chart C illustrates the revenue. Again, at zero output, total revenue is zero. For every unit sold, revenue increases by £200. At 600 units, total revenue amounts to £120 000 (600 × £200). The relationship between revenue and output is also linear and this is reflected in the more rapidly rising total revenue line.

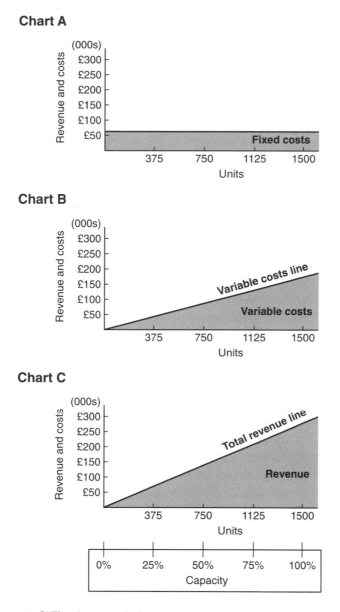

Figure 15.6 The elements of a break-even chart

In Figure 15.7, the three separate charts of Figure 15.6 have been combined to illustrate how the elements work together. First, see the band of *fixed costs* at the base. Positioned above this base is the variable costs wedge. Along the upper boundary of this wedge is the *total cost line*. Finally, the *total revenue line* is shown running from the zero point at zero output and making its way up through the two types of cost until it breaks through the total cost line about half way along. This is the break even point: to the left of it lies loss; to the right profit.

The break even point here occurs at a level of 750 units which equates to revenue of £150 000. Remember from Figure 15.5 that 750 units will result in a contribution of £60 000 (750 × £80), which just equals the fixed cost.

A line is plotted representing the budgeted sales of 1000 units at a unit price of £200. This puts the company a little way to the right of the crucial break even point. The surplus over break even is sometimes referred to as the 'margin of safety'. This *margin of safety* is 25 per cent, which means that sales can fall by this percentage before the break even point is reached.

A number of simplifying assumptions are incorporated in this chart. It has been assumed that fixed costs are totally fixed for *all* levels of output. Also that unit variable costs do not change irrespective of numbers produced and, finally, that unit revenue is the same for all levels of sales. These assumptions may be valid over a fairly narrow range on each side of existing levels of activity. At very low or very high levels, however, the assumptions break down and the chart becomes widely inaccurate.

Notwithstanding these limitations, it is a useful tool for presenting information, for explaining the dynamics of a production unit, for pointing out the essential features of the volume, cost and revenue system and for setting minimum sales targets.

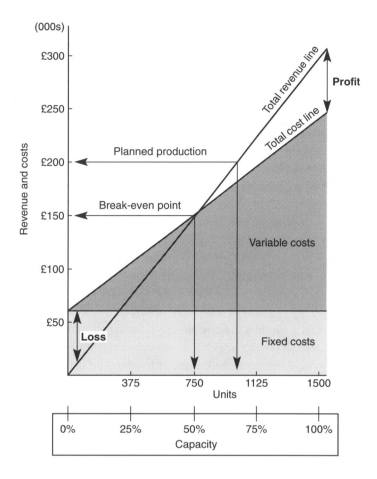

Figure 15.7 Break-even chart for Lawnmowers Ltd

This chart may also be used to identify companies with different cost structures and therefore different levels of what is called *operating leverage*. Operating leverage identifies the change in profit that results from a small change in sales, that is if a 10 per cent change in sales produces a 40 per cent change in profit, then we say that the company has high operating leverage.

Figure 15.8 shows charts for two types of company. The first, (A), has a *high operating leverage*. It has high fixed costs and low unit variable costs, so it has a total cost line that starts high but does not climb steeply. The steep total revenue line cuts the total cost line at quite a wide angle, which means that profit increases rapidly to the right of the break even point. Unfortunately, to the left of this point, the negative gap *also* widens rapidly, meaning that the company gets into heavy losses quickly if output falls below the break even point.

The second, (B), has a *low operating leverage*. This company has low fixed costs but high unit variable costs. The total cost line starts low but climbs steeply with increased volume. The total revenue line produces a much narrower angle at the crossover point, indicating that both profits *and* losses both grow more slowly either right or left of the break even point.

From A we can glean that there is intense pressure to achieve volume sales in order to move out of the heavy loss situation and up to the break even point. When break even is reached, there is the prize of a rapidly increasing profit figure to provide the incentive to achieve even greater volume. When total production capacity exceeds total demand, fierce price competition can erupt between firms of this type as they compete for volume. They are often companies with heavy fixed assets, such as steel production.

The second situation with low operating leverage, is frequently found to exist in companies with smaller, flexible production systems and low fixed assets. These companies tend to have less risk and, but also less reward, attached to them.

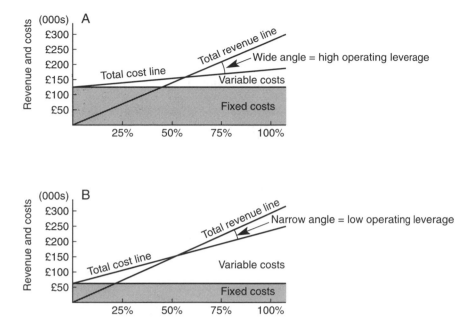

Figure 15.8 Operating leverage

Contribution to sales percentage (CPS)

As noted earlier contribution per unit is limited in its usefulness because it can only be applied to a one-product company. A more general and effective ratio is therefore needed and the following approach is a solution to this problem.

In Figure 15.9 is the familiar diagram of unit selling price, variable costs and contribution. However one extra calculation has been added. *The contribution figure of £80 is expressed as a percentage of the selling price of £200 to give the answer 40 per cent.*

This is a very important percentage and a very important ratio and has several different names in financial literature, such as, profit to volume (PV) ratio. As we have used the term contribution per unit for dealing with units, for consistency we will adopt the term contribution to sales percentage for this ratio in its new form.

This ratio can be used to convert any value of revenue into its corresponding contribution. It can, therefore, be applied to *any* company or any section of a company. It can be used to analyse separate individual products, groups of similar products or the total mix of products for a multi-unit business. When it is used to convert sales into its corresponding contribution, the resulting profit can be derived simply by deducting the fixed costs.

Total contribution

It is important at this point to distinguish between *unit contribution* and *total contribution*. Unit contribution is derived from the selling price minus the variable costs figure. Total contribution can be derived from three separate sources, as shown in Figure 15.11.

- units × CPU
- revenue × CPS
- fixed costs + profit

Figure 15.10 is the same as Figure 15.5 except that contribution to sales percentage has been used in place of contribution per unit. Results are therefore given in money terms rather than in the corresponding units. This form is generally more useful.

As an extra example, consider the following. The budgeted sales for Lawnmowers Ltd is £200 000. Multiply this by 40 per cent to derive the contribution of £80 000. If the revenue figure were to fall to £180 000, then the contribution resulting from that would be £72 000 (£180 000 × 40 per cent). The profit from this reduced level of sales would be £12 000 (£72 000 contribution – £60 000 fixed cost = £12 000 profit).

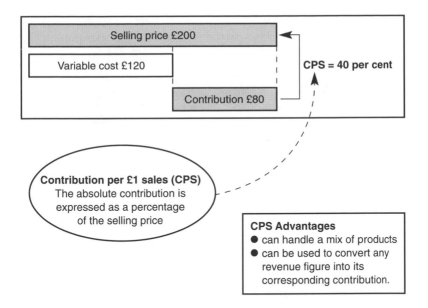

Figure 15.9 Contribution to sales percentage

Basic equation applied to Lawnmowers Ltd figures

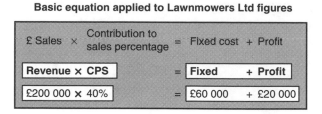

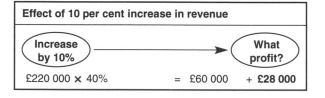

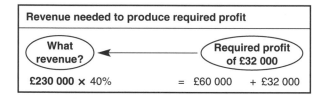

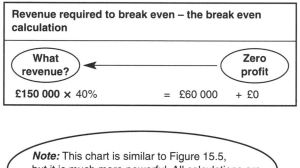

Figure 15.10 Working out the effects of change using the contribution to sales percentage for Lawnmowers Ltd

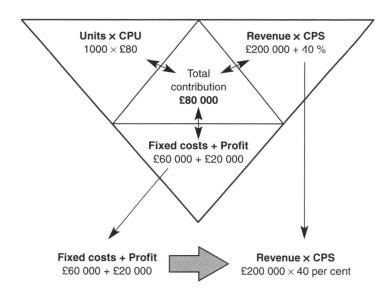

Figure 15.11 Alternative approaches to total contribution

Weighted contribution to sales percentage
We now know how to convert sales into contribution by applying the contribution to sales percentage. Contribution is, therefore, driven by sales. If sales with a constant contribution to sales percentage increase by 10 per cent contribution will increase by the same amount. However we can ask, how constant is this contribution factor? Does it hold across a wide range of products? What drives it?

We know that the ratio is derived from selling price less variable costs expressed as a percentage of the selling price. The selling prices of products are determined not by cost but by the market-place. Most companies do not have the luxury of fixing prices to give secure margins; they must accept or reject, within a range, the generally accepted price. For some products, the prices will be more satisfactory than for others. It is also true that a single product can have more than one price as discounts are given to bulk purchasers and so on. Therefore, the contribution to sales percentage will vary widely for different products and in different markets. The overall contribution to sales percentage is a weighted average of the separate products and markets.

In Figure 15.12 there is an example of a product that is sold direct to the public at a price of £500. It is also sold through agents at a discount of 20 per cent. The variable costs figure in both situations is £350. It can be seen in the first case that the contribution to sales percentage is 30 per cent (£150/£500 × 100) and in the second case that it is 12.5 per cent (£50/£400 × 100).

The third and fourth boxes in Figure 15.12 illustrate the effects that a change in the mix of sales has on the overall weighted average contribution to sales percentage

In the third box, direct sales of £300 000, together with agents' sales of £100 000, give a total contribution of £102 500. The overall weighted average contribution to percentage sales is 25.6 per cent.

In the fourth box, direct sales of £300 000 and agents' sales of £500 000 give a total contribution of £152 500. The overall weighted average contribution to percentage sales is 19 per cent. In this exaggerated example, total sales have doubled in value, but the contribution has only increased by 50 per cent. The weighted average has fallen considerably.

Many companies work on the basis of average values, but it can be dangerous. The average is determined by the mix of high and low contribution products and this mix must be managed. This point is illustrated more fully overleaf.

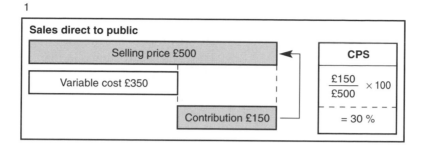

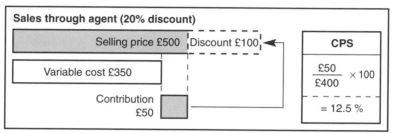

3

Channel	Sales	CPS	Contribution
Direct	£300 000	30%	£90 000
Agent	£100 000	12.5%	£12 500
Total sales	£400 000		£102 500

$$\frac{£102\,500}{£400\,000} \times 100 \longrightarrow \qquad CPS - Average = 25.6\%$$

4

Channel	Sales	CPS	Contribution
Direct	£300 000	30%	£90 000
Agent	£500 000	12.5%	£62 500
Total sales	£800 000		£152 500

$$\frac{£152\,500}{£800\,000} \times 100 \longrightarrow \qquad CPS - Average = 19.0\%$$

Figure 15.12 Overall contribution to sales percentage as a weighted average for a mix of sales

Product mix

In Figure 15.13, data is given about a company that sells three products (A, B and C) through two distribution networks (direct and through agents). There are, therefore, six product market segments, as shown in the matrix in the top left-hand corner. The contribution to sales percentage for each segment is shown in the matrix in the right-hand corner of Figure 15.13.

Budgeted and actual sales of the product market segments are shown beneath these two matrices. Beneath these, the contributions from the two sets of data have been calculated. As shown by the arrows, the sales value in each segment is multiplied by its corresponding contribution to sales percentage to arrive at the contribution for that segment. The contributions from the individual segments are then accumulated to give the total contribution. Fixed costs are £75 000 for both budgeted and actual results and these are deducted to give the final results. A *budgeted profit* of £16 000 has turned into an *actual loss* of £1000.

In comparing budgeted with actual figures, note the following:

- total revenue of £300 000 is unchanged
- selling prices are unchanged
- cost per unit figures are unchanged
- fixed costs are unchanged
- budgeted profit is converted into an actual loss.

The reason for this adverse turnaround can be found in the mix of products. The bulk of sales has moved from high to lower contribution segments. For example, in the bottom right-hand last segment, which has the lowest contribution to sales percentage (Product C sold through agents), sales have increased from a budgeted £20 000 to an actual £60 000. This increase has been offset by reductions in the better segments, and the company has suffered grievously.

Product mix is a potent driver of profit. It must be identified, understood by all and positively managed in order for a business to attain its full potential.

Product/market segments

Products	Product A	Product B	Product C
Distribution			
Direct to customer	✓	✓	✓
Through agent	✓	✓	✓

Contribution to sales percentage

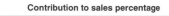

Products	Product A	Product B	Product C
Distribution			
Direct	50%	30%	20%
Agent	30%	20%	10%

Budgeted sales mix	**Actual sales mix**

Sales per segment

Sales	Product A	Product B	Product C
Direct	£70 000	£80 000	£50 000
Agent	£40 000	£40 000	£20 000

Total sales   £300 000

Sales per segment

Sales	Product A	Product B	Product C
Direct	£40 000	£50 000	£50 000
Agent	£30 000	£70 000	£60 000

Total sales   £300 000

Contribution per segment

Contribution	Product A	Product B	Product C
Direct	£35 000	£24 000	£10 000
Agent	£12 000	£8000	£2000

Total contribution   £91 000
Fixed costs   £75 000
Budgeted profit   £16 000

Contribution per segment

Contribution	Product A	Product B	Product C
Direct	£20 000	£15 000	£10 000
Agent	£9000	£14 000	£6000

Total contribution   £74 000
Fixed costs   £75 000
Budgeted profit   (£1000)

Note: A budgeted profit has turned into a loss, notwithstanding the fact that total sales and cost per unit are on target; the product mix has worsened.

Figure 15.13   Product mix analysis

A step beyond contribution to sales percentage

Product mix in terms of contribution to sales percentage by product/market segment is, as noted previouly, a powerful tool that enables management to see how best to use the resources available to it. It is difficult to exaggerate the importance of its proper analysis so as to direct sales *away* from low contribution products towards high contribution areas for a company's financial health.

However, attempting to maximise contribution by means of this technique alone will not always be successful. There are situations in which the promotion of sales of products with high contribution to sales percentage is not to the advantage of the company. This is often true when a company is working at maximum capacity and when different products are competing for this capacity. In such situations, the additional output of one product means lessening output of another.

Consider a manufacturing situation where a high-value machine tool is used to manufacture two products, each of which sells for £5000. Product A has a contribution to sales percentage of 30 per cent while that of product B is 20 per cent. The absolute contribution from product A is £1500 and from product B is £1000.

The selling price to cost relationships of these two products are illustrated in Figure 15.14. From all that has been said so far, it would seem that management should always favour product A over product B. However, it is possible for product B to be *more* profitable than product A. How can this be?

When a company is operating at, or close to, maximum capacity, a further calculation beyond contribution to sales percentage must be done. It is at this point that we come to the concept of **contribution per unit of capacity**. This can be a great identifier of profit so it will be explored overleaf.

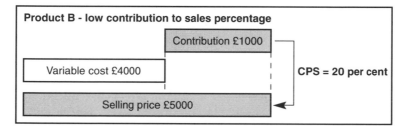

Product A - high contribution to sales percentage

Selling price £5000

Variable cost £3500

Contribution £1500

CPS = 30 percent

Which product is more profitable?
It apears at first sight that product A, with a high value of 30 per cent is a more profitable product for the company than product B with a value of only 20 per cent

Normally this is true, but there are circumstances where product B is more profitable.

We must check its usage of capacity.

Product B - low contribution to sales percentage

Contribution £1000

Variable cost £4000

Selling price £5000

CPS = 20 per cent

Figure 15.14 Selling price to cost relationships of products A and B

Contribution per unit of capacity

Central to Figure 15.15 is an illustration of machine capacity. We will assume that the machine can (after allowing for downtime, maintenance, cleaning and so on) deliver 2000 productive hours per annum. We consider what proportion of this capacity is used by each product, and we then relate this usage of capacity to the total contribution of each product.

Let us look at product A first. One unit of product A takes 10 hours of machine capacity. The total contribution of this unit is £1500. Therefore, the contribution per hour (CPH) of this product is £150. The capacity of the machine remember is 2000 hours per annum, so, at £150 per hour, the maximum contribution attainable from the machine for this product in one year is £300 000.

One unit of product B takes 4 hours of machine capacity. The total contribution of this unit is £1000. Therefore, the CPH of this product is £250. At £250 per hour, the maximum contribution attainable from the machine for this product in one year is £500 000

Product B is, therefore, by far the more profitable product in this situation, *even though* it has a lower contribution to sales percentage. However, the rule applies *only* where capacity is limited and where there is competition between products for this capacity. In this situation contribution will be maximised – and, therefore, so will profit – when activity is directed into those products that have not the highest contribution to sales percentage, but the highest contribution per hour value.

What has been discussed here is a specific instance of the more general case referred to as *contribution per unit of the limiting factor*. The *limiting factor* is the constraint that puts a ceiling on output. Machine hours is the most common limitation, but there can be others, such as raw materials, working capital and so on. Quite often, errors are made in pricing products without reference to this concept, which works greatly to the disadvantage of the company.

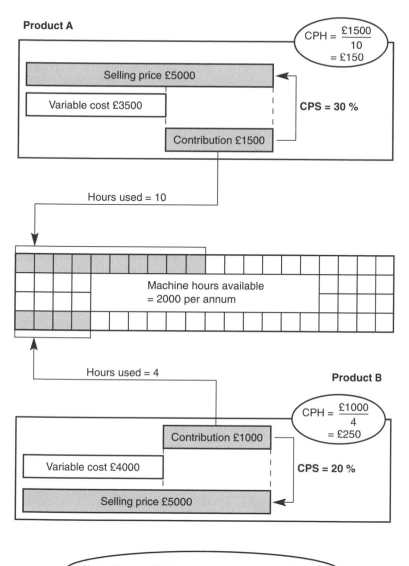

Figure 15.15 Contribution per machine hour of products A and B

16 INVESTMENT RATIOS

INTRODUCTION

The need for a company to earn a return on its investment has been covered in detail. It is clear that this return must meet market expectations if the standing and value of the company is not to suffer.

One of management's critical functions is planning the future of the business to ensure that an adequate rate of return is maintained. Essential to this is adequate new investment as it is the return on this new investment that provides the ongoing profits on which the company depends. Therefore a careful selection process needs to be applied to competing investment proposals so that only the best qualify.

In the past, many approaches have been adopted to assist managers in this selection. One very well tried and tested one that is still in use, is *payback*. Simply calculate the number of years that the project will take to pay back the money invested in it. As a rule of thumb it can provide a useful 'fix' on a project. However, it is not a mathematically sound approach. Some accounting-type measures have also been used in the past that are mathematically suspect.

This chapter is about the sound and tested techniques used now by all major companies to assist them with investment decisions. It illustrates the various measures and ratios that have proved to be effective in selecting and ranking investment projects.

PROJECT APPRAISAL – THE PROBLEM

The standard investment profile shows a large payment up front that the investor hopes will be more than repaid in the form of a stream of payments for a certain number of years. The problem is how to relate the immediate cash outlay accurately to the stream of future repayments.

In A of Figure 16.1, an investment profile is illustrated. All the anticipated repayments could be added up and it would be expected that the total would exceed the initial out-flow, but by *how much* should they exceed it? The sum of the future repayments could be divided by the number of years and this annualised amount could be used as a measure of return. This approach is sometimes adopted but there is something lacking in the answer.

In B, the financial numbers are given for Investment X. The investment is £1000 and the stream of repayments over 5 years add up to £2000. What, then, is the rate of return on the investment (ROI)? The increase in value over the 5 years is 100 per cent, which could be interpreted as 20 per cent per annum. Is this return adequate and how is it affected by inflation? These are the questions investors commonly ask. Before answering them, let us look at one more example.

In C is the example of Investment Y. The investment here is also £1000 and the total of the repayments is also £2000. However, the pattern of repayments is quite different. For each of the first four years, £200 is returned and in Year 5 the initial investment of £1000 plus the usual repayment of £200 is returned. This is the pattern of returns that a 20 per cent fixed interest security would give. The true return on this project is 20 per cent.

When we look back at Investment X, we see that we do not get our investment back in one lump at the end of the period – it is spread over each year. The yearly cash repayments, then, are both paying interest on the investments *and* repaying the principal. This is the pattern of returns given by commercial investments. The return to the investor here cannot be assessed easily.

A

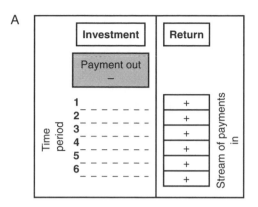

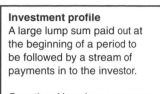

Investment profile
A large lump sum paid out at the beginning of a period to be followed by a stream of payments in to the investor.

Question: How do we compare the stream with the lump sum?

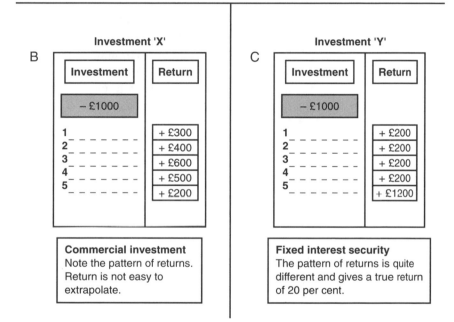

Commercial investment
Note the pattern of returns. Return is not easy to extrapolate.

Fixed interest security
The pattern of returns is quite different and gives a true return of 20 per cent.

Figure 16.1 Investment profiles

PROJECT APPRAISAL – STEPS TO A SOLUTION

In Section A of Figure 16.2, the diagrammatic layout of the investment appraisal problem in the top left-hand corner is the same as in Figure 16.1, but here it is developed further. Each future payment is connected by an arrow back to the present time, showing that it is necessary to convert future payments into present-day values. The sum of these present values will give a total that can be directly related to the investment amount. We can now compare like with like and have more trust in the results.

In Section B in the figure, a mechanism is laid out that makes it possible to take into account the effect of time on the value of money. Centrally placed is the box showing £100 which is aligned with the time period zero. Periods going forward into the future and back into the past are shown on the right- and left-hand sides of zero respectively. An interest rate of 10 per cent is used here to keep things simple. As we move to the right of the central zero point, the interest factors given are 1.100, 1.210 and 1.331, which is 10 per cent compounded for years +1, +2 and +3. Applied to the sum of £100 they tell us that the equivalent of £100 in today's terms is £133.1 at the end of Year 3. To the left of the model, the factors are 0.909, 0.826 and 0.751. This last one tells us that £100 carried back 3 Years has a value of £75.1.

This stream of factors on the left and right express the impact of time on money. These factors are used to give a weighting to the time period in which each cash movement occurs.

The investment appraisal technique relies mainly on the factors to the left of centre, that is the discount factors, but some versions also use the right-hand factors. To carry out our analysis we can select any interest rate we wish. A higher rate would give a lower discount factor and vice versa. (*See* Appendix 3 for relevant interest rate tables.) We can calculate the present or future value of any sum of money due in any period past or future by using such tables.

To analyse the return from an investment one starts with a stream of cash flows and converts each item separately to its present value. An arrow shows how the discount factor for 3 years at 10% ie .751, is applied to a cash flow in year 3 to give its equivalent value at the time the investment is made. Then these separate amounts are aggregated into one sum. This sum is then compared directly with the investment amount so that an investment decision can be made.

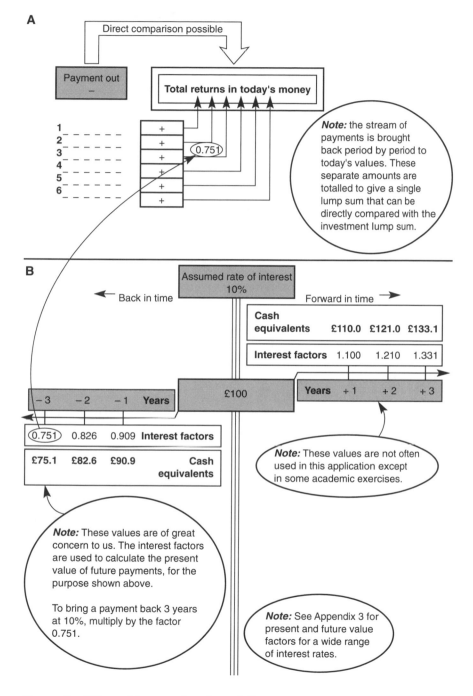

Figure 16.2 Effects of time on value of a cash flow

PROJECT APPRAISAL – PRESENT VALUE (PV)

Figure 16.3 shows a three-year example of a project as follows:

- an investment of £5000
- return in Year 1 of £1500, Year 2 of £3500 and Year 3 of £1400.

We wish to ascertain if the rate of return on this investment is 10 per cent. We see the method for setting out the problem and how the 10 per cent discount factors are applied to the stream of returns. The present value of each conversion is shown together with the summarised sum, £5309. The technical name for this amount of £5309 is the present value (PV).

What information can be drawn from the relationship between the investment amount of £5000 and the present value of £5309? To answer this question we will examine the meaning of the present value figure.

B in the diagram demonstrates the relationship between the value £5309 and the stream of income from the investment. It considers £5309 to be a loan from the bank for 3 years at 10 per cent. The loan schedule shows the interest charged to the account by the bank each year and the repayments by the client. These repayments match the stream of income from the project. *The repayments totally clear off the loan that carries an interest rate of 10 per cent.* To clarify this relationship further, the column headed 'Bank cash movements' shows that the loan of £5309 is exactly balanced by the project's stream of income while, at the same time, the bank *earned 10 per cent on the amount of the loan outstanding at any time.* Note that the bank does not earn 10 per cent interest on *£5309 for 3 years*, but only on the *outstanding balance each year*.

This example establishes the meaning of present value: it is the sum of money today that exactly matches a future stream of income at a given rate of interest. A higher rate of interest produces a lower present value. In answer to the question posed earlier in this section, an investment of £5309 would earn *exactly* 10 per cent, so *more* than 10 per cent would be earned by the smaller investment of £5000.

Example project tested at 10 per cent

A

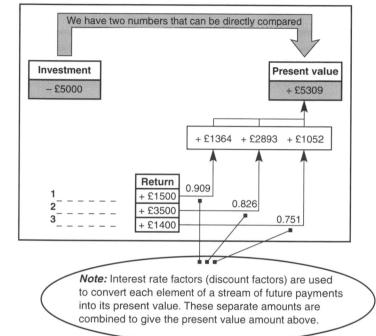

We have two numbers that can be directly compared

Investment
− £5000

Present value
+ £5309

+ £1364   + £2893   + £1052

Return
+ £1500
+ £3500
+ £1400

1 — — — —
2 — — — —
3 — — — —

0.909
0.826
0.751

Note: Interest rate factors (discount factors) are used to convert each element of a stream of future payments into its present value. These separate amounts are combined to give the present value amount above.

We use a bank loan example below to illustrate the relationship between the present value calculated above and the stream of income.

B

Loan schedule

Bank cash movements

| Bank loan at 10 per cent | £5309 | → | − £5309 |

End Year 1	Interest @ 10%	£530
	Total due	£5839
	Repayment	£1500	→ + £1500
	Balance	**£4339**

End Year 2	Interest @ 10%	£434
	Total due	£4773
	Repayment	£3500	→ + £3500
	Balance	**£1273**

End Year 3	Interest @ 10%	£127
	Total due	£1400
	Repayment	£1400	→ + £1400
	Balance	**0**

This cash flow yields exactly 10% to the bank. It proves that the present value of £5309 equates exactly to the stream of cash inflows £1500; £3500; £1400, at the 10% interest rate.

Figure 16.3 Calculating present value

PROJECT APPRAISAL – INTERNAL RATE OF RETURN (IRR)

The previous example has shown that the investment of £5000 earns more than 10 per cent. When the present value exceeds the investment amount, it can be concluded that the rate of return is greater than the interest rate used in the calculation. However, we do not know what *actual* rate of return is being delivered by the project. Unfortunately, there is no mathematical way of going directly to the answer. Instead, a series of tests, at various rates, must be carried out. In A in Figure 16.4 a second test is carried out at 11 per cent. The present value here is £5216. This present value, again, is greater than the investment, so it can be concluded that the return also exceeds 11 per cent.

In B, at interest rates between 10 per cent and 15 per cent as listed in column 1. In the second column the present values that correspond to the different discount rates are £5309, £5216, £5126 and so on. Note how these amounts fall in value as higher interest rates are applied. The third column has the unchanged investment figure of £5000 in all rows. The fourth column introduces a new term – net present value (NPV). This value is derived by deducting the investment from the present value.

The net present value at 10 per cent is £309 (positive) and at 11 per cent it is £216 (positive). Going down the column, the value remains positive as far as 13 per cent. At 14 per cent it becomes negative. It is, of course, even more negative at 15 per cent. It can be concluded from these values, then, that the investment is earning *more than 13 per cent and less than 14 per cent*. At approximately 13.5 per cent, the value in the net present value column would equal zero. This value of 13.5 per cent is the rate of return being earned by the project. It is referred to as the internal rate of return (IRR). *Definition:* The IRR is the rate that makes the present value of the stream of returns exactly equal the investment.

A

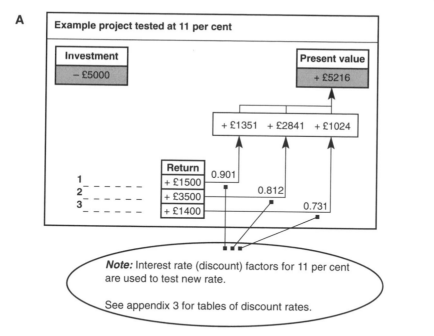

Example project tested at 11 per cent

Investment		Present value
− £5000		+ £5216

+ £1351   + £2841   + £1024

Return		0.901
1	+ £1500	
2	+ £3500	0.812
3	+ £1400	0.731

Note: Interest rate (discount) factors for 11 per cent are used to test new rate.

See appendix 3 for tables of discount rates.

B   **Schedule of tests at different interest rates**

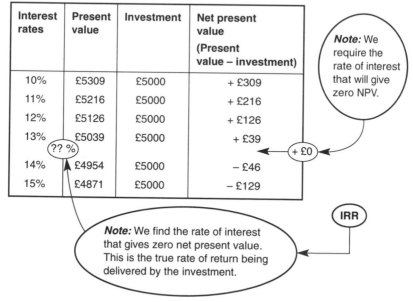

Interest rates	Present value	Investment	Net present value (Present value – investment)
10%	£5309	£5000	+ £309
11%	£5216	£5000	+ £216
12%	£5126	£5000	+ £126
13%	£5039	£5000	+ £39
?? %			+ £0
14%	£4954	£5000	− £46
15%	£4871	£5000	− £129

Note: We require the rate of interest that will give zero NPV.

Note: We find the rate of interest that gives zero net present value. This is the true rate of return being delivered by the investment.

IRR

Figure 16.4 Calculating the internal rate of return

PROJECT APPRAISAL – SUMMARY

The technique of investment appraisal that has been described is called discounted cash flow (DCF) (*see* Figure 16.5). To apply this technique the cash flow, positive or negative, for each time period must first be identified. Then, one or both of the approaches illustrated is used:

The net present value method:
- select the required rate of interest (*see* below)
- apply it to the stream of cash flows to derive net present value
- if net present value is positive, select the project, otherwise do not.

Internal rate of return
- find the interest rate that makes net present value equal to zero
- if this rate is satisfactory, select project, otherwise do not.

All we have considered in this chapter is how to do the mathematical calculations after we have established what the cash flows from a project will be. In practical terms, managers will not have to physically do the calculations because computer programs are everywhere and they will do this for them. However, it is necessary for a manager to formulate the problem correctly and to interpret the various ratios produced in order to make sound decisions based on more than guesswork.

Figure 16.5 gives an outline structure for analysing investment decisions problems. The four elements within the overall structure are:

- cost of the investments
- annual returns
- life of project
- rate of return.

The area for which it is hardest to obtain reliable data is annual returns. There are no rules for this. Common sense and business acumen must apply here. It is normal to test a series of scenarios to examine the sensitivity of the project to small changes in input variables. Over time the accuracy of predictions can be monitored and suitable filtering mechanisms can be adopted as necessary.

Discounted cash flow

Cash flow is used to measure the return on investment rather than profit because:

- it is easier to identify in respect of a single project and
- mathematically, it is more correct.

The four separate elements that have to be quantified are as follows

Cost of the investment
This is probably the easiest amount to establish. Consider incremental cash outlay only, that is the total extra cash out-flow that results from implementing this project as opposed to not doing it. Allow for any savings, such as tax. Remember to include working capital outlays, such as extra inventories associated with the project. Do not add in any allocated costs, that is costs transferred from another part of the organisation which do not give rise to any extra cash out-flow.

Annual returns from the project
The appropriate figure for each period is the incremental cash in-flow after tax. This value is derived from the extra revenue to be received less the extra cash costs to be incurred. Do not include any allocated costs in the calculations.

Life of the project
The number of years can be determined by the project's physical, technological or economical life span: a heavy-duty vehicle has a physical life of five years, a computer could have a physical life of 25 years but a technological life of three years and so on. For very long-life projects, for example an hotel, look out a maximum of six to eight years and assume a terminal value at the end of that time. This is treated as a cash in-flow in the final year of the analysis.

Rate of return
This can be a contentious issue, related as it is to the cost of capital. In practice, a rate is laid down by the policy makers in the business. It is a rate that all new projects are expected to exceed. It is often called the 'hurdle rate' for this reason. To allow for different levels of risk in projects, different discount rates may be applied.

Figure 16.5 Discounted cash flow – the component parts

APPENDIX ONE
Special items

ITEMS OF SPECIAL INTEREST

Values taken from company accounts are used to analyse business performance. For the vast bulk of these values there are no quibbles about their
accuracy or realism. However, there are some items that are subject to a
number of different interpretations. Whether one interpretation is preferred
over another will affect the results of the analysis. A multitude of rules laid
down by the accounting bodies, the statutory authorities, the Stock
Exchange and others have a bearing in these interpretations. Some understanding of the more important of these rules provides a useful background
to analysis.

The principle underlying the rules may be even more important. The
overriding principle is the 'true and fair view' that accounts should present.
This said, it is often difficult to draw up rules for specific items that will
always reflect a true and fair view. It is for this reason that different interpretations can arise to give different answers to our analysis.

As external conditions change, the emphasis moves to different aspects
of the accounts – from the profit and loss account to the balance sheet to the
cash flow. New problems, such as fluctuating currencies, give rise to the
need for new rules and so on. This appendix will address some of the more
important 'live' issues in accounting at the present time. It will explain *why*
they are live, what the current state of play is and how different methods of
treatment would affect the analysis. These issues are:

- goodwill
- foreign currencies
- pensions
- deferred tax
- leases
- revaluation of fixed assets
- scrip issues
- miscellaneous long funds.

GOODWILL ON ACQUISITION

When one company acquires another for a price (consideration) in excess of its net assets, goodwill is created. This goodwill amount will appear not in the accounts of either the buyer or vendor, but in the consolidated, or, combined accounts of the two companies. Goodwill is called an *intangible asset*, that is an asset of no physical substance. In many ratios, calculations are based on tangible assets only, thus totally ignoring goodwill. Nevertheless, it has important effects on a company's reported position and so an understanding of its origins and treatment is important.

First we will look at a non-goodwill situation called Scenario 1 in Figure A1.1. It will serve as a base position from which to work towards a goodwill example.

Company A has paid £100 for Company B, the balance sheet for which is shown with a net worth of £100. The entries that appear in Company A's balance sheet are 'Investment £100' and the investment is balanced by an equivalent long term loan.

When we look at the consolidated balance sheet for Scenario 1 the item 'Investment £100' has disappeared. The values in the following boxes are combined:

- fixed assets
- current assets
- current liabilities
- long-term loans.

The ordinary funds of Company A are unchanged in the consolidated balance sheet. Also, before consolidation, the total assets were £1000 for A and £400 for B. The combined statement is in balance with its total assets being equal to the sum of the two separate companies less the Company A £100 investment and Company B ordinary funds deducted from each side.

When we consider what has happened, we see that the investment of £100 in Company A's balance sheet has simply been replaced by net assets of £100 (£400 assets – £300 liabilities) from Company B.

In practice, the question of 'fair value' of both assets acquired and consideration given would arise. It has been assumed that this is not an issue here.

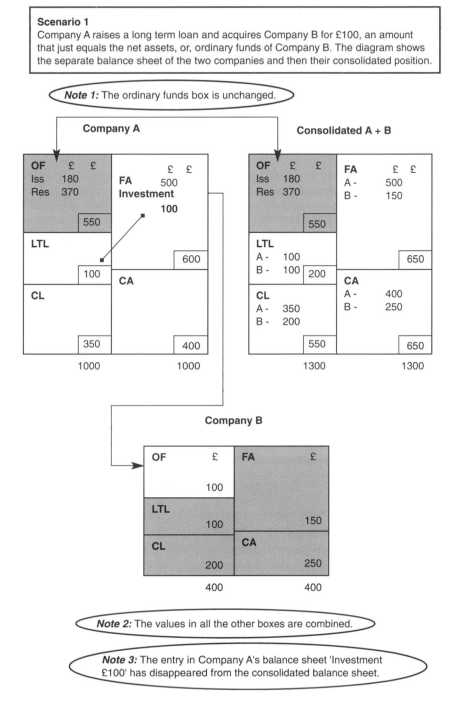

Figure *AI.I Non-goodwill acquisition*

A goodwill acquisition

In Scenario 2 in Figure A1.2, the amount paid by Company A for Company B is £125. Company B is the same firm as in Scenario 1, whose net assets are £100. On consolidation, the extra consideration of £25 is not balanced by physical assets so an *intangible asset* of this amount must be created. The name we give to this intangible asset is *goodwill*. (The justification for a high acquisition price and, therefore, the goodwill element, exists in the mind of the buyer, but, logically, it has to be the expectation of extra future profit.)

Once consideration in cash or other assets is given for goodwill, a number of questions then arise:

- 'How is it treated in the accounts?'
- 'How will different ways of treating it affect our analysis?'

Two ways of treating goodwill are:

- by annual charges to the profit and loss account – it can be depreciated in just the same way as any fixed assets and it will, in time, disappear from the accounts (this way out is not favoured by business people because its effect is to reduce declared profit, which will be reflected in the earnings per share figure and other measures of performance).
- by an immediate charge against reserves – assets may be reduced by the amount of goodwill and reserves by the same amount so, at a single stroke, goodwill simply disappears, totally (in the consolidated balance sheet shown in Figure A1.2, reserves of £370 would be reduced by £25 to £345, reported ordinary funds would fall by £25 to £525 and balance sheet totals go down to £1300).

The effect of the second treatment is that profits are not affected and various balance sheet totals are reduced. Because of higher profits and lower assets the profitability ratios of return on total assets and return on equity will look better. The debt/equity ratio, though, will look worse because equity funds are artificially reduced. It is likely that the high return on total assets, return on equity, and market to book ratios in the FT-SE Companies 1990 are partly attributable to this treatment of goodwill.

Scenario 2
Company A raises a long term loan and acquires Company B for £125, an amount that exceeds the net assets, or, ordinary funds of Company B by £25. The diagram shows the separate balance sheet of the two companies and then their consolidated position.

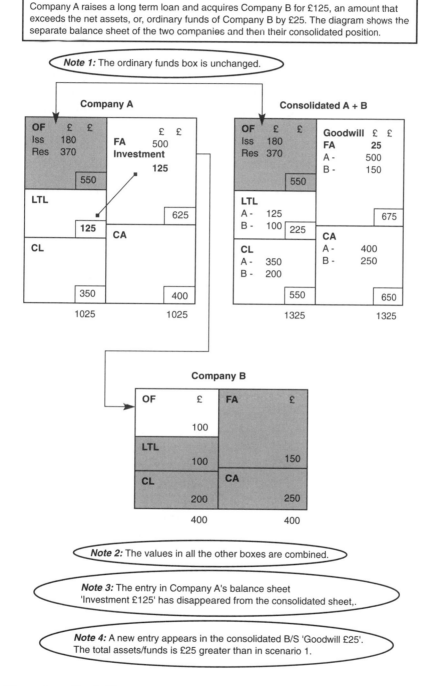

Note 1: The ordinary funds box is unchanged.

Company A

OF	£	£		£	£
Iss	180		FA	500	
Res	370		Investment		
				125	
		550			
LTL					
					625
		125	CA		
CL					
		350			400
		1025			1025

Consolidated A + B

OF	£	£	Goodwill	£	£
Iss	180		FA		25
Res	370		A -		500
			B -		150
		550			
LTL					
A -	125				675
B -	100	225	CA		
CL			A -		400
A -	350		B -		250
B -	200				
		550			650
		1325			1325

Company B

OF	£	FA	£
	100		
LTL			
	100		150
CL		CA	
	200		250
	400		400

Note 2: The values in all the other boxes are combined.

Note 3: The entry in Company A's balance sheet 'Investment £125' has disappeared from the consolidated sheet,.

Note 4: A new entry appears in the consolidated B/S 'Goodwill £25'. The total assets/funds is £25 greater than in scenario 1.

Figure A1.2 Goodwill on acquisition

FOREIGN CURRENCY

Movements in exchange rates affect company performance in various ways, principally by way of transactions in the profit and loss account and holdings of overseas assets and liabilities in the balance sheet. We often note that an increase in the value of sterling will cause a weakening in the share price of companies with substantial foreign interests, and vice versa.

In general, gains and losses arising from foreign currency exchange rate movements are treated as follows:

- profit and loss transactions are translated at average currency values for the year
- assets and liabilities in the closing balance sheet are translated at rates that applied at the date of the final accounts.
- net assets of the opening balance sheet are restated at the closing rates the difference from the previous year being taken to reserves
- exchange differences on foreign currency borrowings directly raised for, or to provide a hedge against, overseas fixed assets are taken to reserves and offset against the exchange differences on the assets.
- all other gains and losses are passed through the profit and loss account.

PENSIONS

Capital sums invested in pension funds and annual contributions have grown so large that they can have a bearing on company performance. The pension funds themselves should not directly impinge on a company's accounts because they are separate funds totally independent of company finances. However, the liability of a company to provide for employees' pensions means that a shortfall in the fund has to be filled by increased annual contributions. Likewise, a surplus can allow the company to take a holiday from contributions, thereby improving its cash flow and profit results. The surplus or deficit on the fund is, therefore, of supreme importance to the value of the company.

DEFERRED TAX

The amount of tax *charged* in company accounts is often considerably different from the actual tax *paid*. This arises from 'timing differences that are likely to reverse in the foreseeable future'. Behind this phrase lies government legislation. To encourage investment in fixed assets, many governments give accelerated capital allowances on new plant. They allow a higher charge against profits for the writing down of the fixed assets than would be justified on the basis of a straightforward depreciation calculation.

The result to the company is a lower tax charge in the early years of an investment. However, if excess amounts are taken for depreciation early in the life of plant, there is none left for later years. The result will be heavier tax charges in these latter years. It is accepted that, for business purposes, this artificial distortion of reported profits is better avoided. Accordingly, in the early years, the full tax charge is made in the accounts and the amount not paid is put to the deferred tax account. It will be drawn down in later years. However, this said, a certain amount is left to the discretion of management to determine how much of a charge is 'likely to crystallise in the foreseeable future'.

FINANCE LEASES

Assets in the balance sheet include only items that are owned by the company. At least, this was the fundamental rule until quite recently when a considerable amount of *off-balance sheet financing* came into use. By this phrase is meant that assets were being acquired which were funded by loans, but neither the asset nor the loan appeared in the accounts. In legal terms, these assets were leased, but all the risks and rewards of ownership accrued to the company. The term *finance lease* is now used in this situation to distinguish it from the ordinary operating lease. With a finance lease, both the asset and the funding must appear in the accounts.

REVALUATION OF FIXED ASSETS

High rates of inflation over two decades had resulted in a situation where the values for property in company accounts were far removed from reality. It was accepted that it was necessary to remove this anomaly and fixed assets were allowed to be shown at valuation rather than at cost.

Our interest here is to consider the effect of revaluation on the various business ratios. First we will look at the accounting treatment that is illustrated in Figure A1.3. The increase in value of the fixed assets is matched by an increase in reserves.

Balance sheet values for fixed assets, total assets and ordinary funds are increased. The impact on business ratios is exactly the opposite to that which resulted from the writing off of goodwill shown earlier in this appendix. The debt/equity ratio improves, as does the asset backing per share. However, return on total assets and return on equity will worsen. For an analysis of accounts for a series of years, spurious movements in ratios can arise simply from revaluation. The best way to eliminate these is to back-date the revaluation to the start of the analysis period.

Balance sheet (before revaluation)   **Balance sheet** (after revaluation)

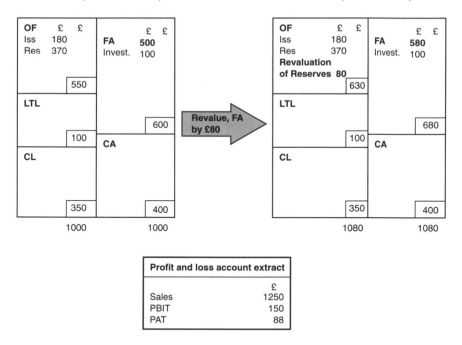

Profit and loss account extract	
	£
Sales	1250
PBIT	150
PAT	88

Ratios	Before	After	
ROTA	15%	13.9%	**Worse**
ROE	16%	14%	**Worse**
D/E	82%	71%	**Better**

Figure A1.3 Revaluation of fixed assets

SCRIP ISSUE

A *scrip,* or, *bonus issue* takes place when shareholders in a company are given extra free shares in proportion to their existing holdings. For instance in a *one-for-two scrip*, all shareholders will have their number of shares increased by 50 per cent. From a ratio point of view, this has an effect on EPS, DPS, assets per share and, normally, market price per share. The historic values must all be moved down in proportion to the increase in number of shares.

Does a scrip bring real benefit to the shareholder? The logic is that there should be *no* change in their overall position: they own the same fraction of the company after the scrip as before and the total value of the company has not increased. However, in practice, a scrip is a buoyant signal to the market that may improve a share's value. The accounting entry is simply a transfer from reserves to issued reserves, as shown in Figure A1.4.

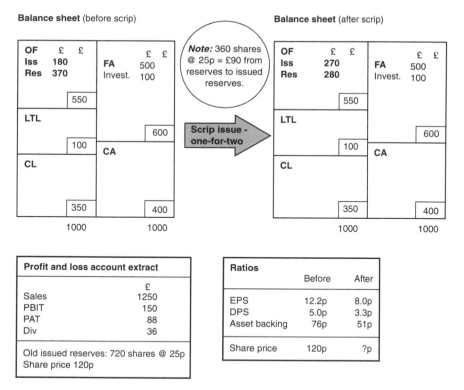

Balance sheet (before scrip)

OF	£	£			£	£
Iss	180		FA		500	
Res	370		Invest.		100	
		550				
LTL						600
		100	CA			
CL						
		350				400
		1000				1000

Note: 360 shares @ 25p = £90 from reserves to issued reserves.

Scrip issue - one-for-two

Balance sheet (after scrip)

OF	£	£			£	£
Iss	270		FA		500	
Res	280		Invest.		100	
		550				
LTL						600
		100	CA			
CL						
		350				400
		1000				1000

Profit and loss account extract	
	£
Sales	1250
PBIT	150
PAT	88
Div	36
Old issued reserves: 720 shares @ 25p Share price 120p	

Ratios	Before	After
EPS	12.2p	8.0p
DPS	5.0p	3.3p
Asset backing	76p	51p
Share price	120p	?p

Figure A1.4 Effects of a scrip issue on the accounts

MISCELLANEOUS LONG-TERM FUNDS

In Chapter 1 it was mentioned that certain items do not fit comfortably into the structure of the five-box balance sheet. These items have been ignored throughout the analysis in this book because, in many companies, these items do not exist at all and in most others, they are of little importance from a financial analysis point of view. However, they are mentioned here as an aside so that when they *are* encountered they can be dealt with appropriately. Figure A1.5 shows their location in the balance sheet. Under the heading 'Miscellaneous long-term funds', they lie between ordinary funds and long term loans.

Preference shares

Preference shareholders paradoxically, have very limited rights. They are part-owners and receive a dividend at a fixed per cent before the ordinary shareholder. At one time this was a popular form of funding, but it is now used in very limited and special circumstances. It may be for tax planning or voting control purposes for example. Preference shares will often have conversion rights into ordinary shares and, if so, they can be included with that category. For debt/equity ratio purposes, they can be treated as equity.

Minority interests

This entry occurs when the consolidated group includes subsidiaries that are less than 100 per cent owned. They are equity funds but not part of the group's equity. Usually the amount is insignificant, but, for calculating the debt/equity ratio, they could, again, be included with equity.

Deferred tax, grants and miscellaneous provisions

Deferred tax has been discussed above. It is probably best treated as an 'interest-free loan' from the government and, therefore, included as debt. Grants will, in due course, move up into equity. Miscellaneous provisions could be pension funds not fully covered; they are neither debt nor equity. Both items can be ignored in the balance sheet ratios unless the amounts are significant. For FT-SE Companies these items combined amount to 9 per cent approximately of the balance sheet, but had been allocated to either debt or equity in our earlier illustrations. In Figure 10.5 the debt to total assets percentage that appears to be 54 per cent from the simplified balance sheet comes out at 47 per cent when these miscellaneous items are stripped away.

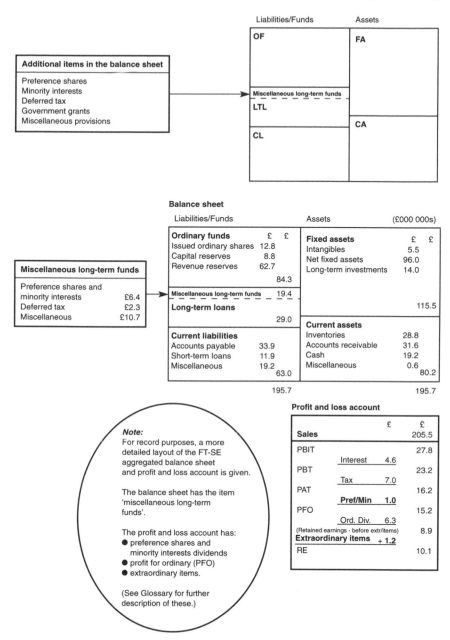

Figure A1.5 Entering miscellaneous long-term funds into the account for the FT-SE Companies 1990

APPENDIX TWO
FT-SE Companies 1990

List of the companies from the FT-SE 100 Share Index used in summary accounts.

Allied Lyons PLC
Argyll Group PLC
Associated British Foods PLC
BAA PLC
BET PLC
Blue Circle Industries PLC
BOC Group PLC
Boots Company (The) PLC
British Aerospace PLC
British Telecommunications PLC
BTR PLC
Cable and Wireless PLC
Cadbury Schweppes PLC
Courtaulds PLC
Fisons PLC
Forte PLC
General Electric Co. PLC
Glaxo Holdings PLC
Great Universal Stores PLC
Guinness PLC
Hanson PLC
Hillsdown Holdings PLC
Imperial Chemical Industries PLC
Inchcape PLC
Kingfisher PLC
Ladbroke Group PLC
Laporte PLC
Lonrho PLC
Marks and Spencer PLC
NFC PLC

Northern Foods PLC
Pearson PLC
Pilkington PLC
Rank Organisation (The) PLC
Reckitt and Colman PLC
Redland PLC
Reed International PLC
Rentokil Group PLC
Reuters Holdings PLC
RMC Group PLC
Rolls Royce PLC
Rothmans International PLC
Sainsbury (J) PLC
Scottish and Newcastle Breweries PLC
Sears PLC
Smith & Nephew PLC
Smith (WH) Group PLC
Tarmac PLC
Tate and Lyle PLC
Tesco PLC
Thorn EMI PLC
Tomkins PLC
Trafalgar House PLC
Unilever
United Biscuits (Holdings) PLC
Wellcome PLC
Whitbread PLC
Williams Holdings PLC

APPENDIX THREE
Discounting and compounding tables

Present value of £1

Years	1%	2%	3%	4%	5%	6%	7%	8%	9%	10%	11%	12%
1	0.990	0.980	0.971	0.962	0.952	0.943	0.935	0.926	0.917	0.909	0.901	0.893
2	0.980	0.961	0.943	0.925	0.907	0.890	0.873	0.857	0.842	0.826	0.812	0.797
3	0.971	0.942	0.915	0.889	0.864	0.840	0.816	0.794	0.772	0.751	0.731	0.712
4	0.961	0.924	0.888	0.855	0.823	0.792	0.763	0.735	0.708	0.683	0.659	0.636
5	0.951	0.906	0.863	0.822	0.784	0.747	0.713	0.681	0.650	0.621	0.593	0.567
6	0.942	0.888	0.837	0.790	0.746	0.705	0.666	0.630	0.596	0.564	0.535	0.507
7	0.933	0.871	0.813	0.760	0.711	0.665	0.623	0.583	0.547	0.513	0.482	0.452
8	0.923	0.853	0.789	0.731	0.677	0.627	0.582	0.540	0.502	0.467	0.434	0.404
9	0.914	0.837	0.766	0.703	0.645	0.592	0.544	0.500	0.460	0.424	0.391	0.361
10	0.905	0.820	0.744	0.676	0.614	0.558	0.508	0.463	0.422	0.386	0.352	0.322
11	0.896	0.804	0.722	0.650	0.585	0.527	0.475	0.429	0.388	0.350	0.317	0.287
12	0.887	0.788	0.701	0.625	0.557	0.497	0.444	0.397	0.356	0.319	0.286	0.257
13	0.879	0.773	0.681	0.601	0.530	0.469	0.415	0.368	0.326	0.290	0.258	0.229
14	0.870	0.758	0.661	0.577	0.505	0.442	0.388	0.340	0.299	0.263	0.232	0.205
15	0.861	0.743	0.642	0.555	0.481	0.417	0.362	0.315	0.275	0.239	0.209	0.183
16	0.853	0.728	0.623	0.534	0.458	0.394	0.339	0.292	0.252	0.218	0.188	0.163
17	0.844	0.714	0.605	0.513	0.436	0.371	0.317	0.270	0.231	0.198	0.170	0.146
18	0.836	0.700	0.587	0.494	0.416	0.350	0.296	0.250	0.212	0.180	0.153	0.130
19	0.828	0.686	0.570	0.475	0.396	0.331	0.277	0.232	0.194	0.164	0.138	0.116
20	0.820	0.673	0.554	0.456	0.377	0.312	0.258	0.215	0.178	0.149	0.124	0.104
21	0.811	0.660	0.538	0.439	0.359	0.294	0.242	0.199	0.164	0.135	0.112	0.093
22	0.803	0.647	0.522	0.422	0.342	0.278	0.226	0.184	0.150	0.123	0.101	0.083
23	0.795	0.634	0.507	0.406	0.326	0.262	0.211	0.170	0.138	0.112	0.091	0.074
24	0.788	0.622	0.492	0.390	0.310	0.247	0.197	0.158	0.126	0.102	0.082	0.066
25	0.780	0.610	0.478	0.375	0.295	0.233	0.184	0.146	0.116	0.092	0.074	0.059
26	0.772	0.598	0.464	0.361	0.281	0.220	0.172	0.135	0.106	0.084	0.066	0.053
27	0.764	0.586	0.450	0.347	0.268	0.207	0.161	0.125	0.098	0.076	0.060	0.047
28	0.757	0.574	0.437	0.333	0.255	0.196	0.150	0.116	0.090	0.069	0.054	0.042
29	0.749	0.563	0.424	0.321	0.243	0.185	0.141	0.107	0.082	0.063	0.048	0.037
30	0.742	0.552	0.412	0.308	0.231	0.174	0.131	0.099	0.075	0.057	0.044	0.033

Note: To convert £1 in the future into a present value apply the factor that matches both the number of years and the interest rate, for example, 6 years, 4 per cent = £0.790.

Present value of £1

Years	13%	14%	15%	16%	17%	18%	19%	20%	21%	22%	23%	24%
1	0.885	0.877	0.870	0.862	0.855	0.847	0.840	0.833	0.826	0.820	0.813	0.806
2	0.783	0.769	0.756	0.743	0.731	0.718	0.706	0.694	0.683	0.672	0.661	0.650
3	0.693	0.675	0.658	0.641	0.624	0.609	0.593	0.579	0.564	0.551	0.537	0.524
4	0.613	0.592	0.572	0.552	0.534	0.516	0.499	0.482	0.467	0.451	0.437	0.423
5	0.543	0.519	0.497	0.476	0.456	0.437	0.419	0.402	0.386	0.370	0.355	0.341
6	0.480	0.456	0.432	0.410	0.390	0.370	0.352	0.335	0.319	0.303	0.289	0.275
7	0.425	0.400	0.376	0.354	0.333	0.314	0.296	0.279	0.263	0.249	0.235	0.222
8	0.376	0.351	0.327	0.305	0.285	0.266	0.249	0.233	0.218	0.204	0.191	0.179
9	0.333	0.308	0.284	0.263	0.243	0.225	0.209	0.194	0.180	0.167	0.155	0.144
10	0.295	0.270	0.247	0.227	0.208	0.191	0.176	0.162	0.149	0.137	0.126	0.116
11	0.261	0.237	0.215	0.195	0.178	0.162	0.148	0.135	0.123	0.112	0.103	0.094
12	0.231	0.208	0.187	0.168	0.152	0.137	0.124	0.112	0.102	0.092	0.083	0.076
13	0.204	0.182	0.163	0.145	0.130	0.116	0.104	0.093	0.084	0.075	0.068	0.061
14	0.181	0.160	0.141	0.125	0.111	0.099	0.088	0.078	0.069	0.062	0.055	0.049
15	0.160	0.140	0.123	0.108	0.095	0.084	0.074	0.065	0.057	0.051	0.045	0.040
16	0.141	0.123	0.107	0.093	0.081	0.071	0.062	0.054	0.047	0.042	0.036	0.032
17	0.125	0.108	0.093	0.080	0.069	0.060	0.052	0.045	0.039	0.034	0.030	0.026
18	0.111	0.095	0.081	0.069	0.059	0.051	0.044	0.038	0.032	0.028	0.024	0.021
19	0.098	0.083	0.070	0.060	0.051	0.043	0.037	0.031	0.027	0.023	0.020	0.017
20	0.087	0.073	0.061	0.051	0.043	0.037	0.031	0.026	0.022	0.019	0.016	0.014
21	0.077	0.064	0.053	0.044	0.037	0.031	0.026	0.022	0.018	0.015	0.013	0.011
22	0.068	0.056	0.046	0.038	0.032	0.026	0.022	0.018	0.015	0.013	0.011	0.009
23	0.060	0.049	0.040	0.033	0.027	0.022	0.018	0.015	0.012	0.010	0.009	0.007
24	0.053	0.043	0.035	0.028	0.023	0.019	0.015	0.013	0.010	0.008	0.007	0.006
25	0.047	0.038	0.030	0.024	0.020	0.016	0.013	0.010	0.009	0.007	0.006	0.005
26	0.042	0.033	0.026	0.021	0.017	0.014	0.011	0.009	0.007	0.006	0.005	0.004
27	0.037	0.029	0.023	0.018	0.014	0.011	0.009	0.007	0.006	0.005	0.004	0.003
28	0.033	0.026	0.020	0.016	0.012	0.010	0.008	0.006	0.005	0.004	0.003	0.002
29	0.029	0.022	0.017	0.014	0.011	0.008	0.006	0.005	0.004	0.003	0.002	0.002
30	0.026	0.020	0.015	0.012	0.009	0.007	0.005	0.004	0.003	0.003	0.002	0.002

Present value of annuity of £1

Years	1%	2%	3%	4%	5%	6%	7%	8%	9%	10%	11%	12%
1	0.990	0.980	0.971	0.962	0.952	0.943	0.935	0.926	0.917	0.909	0.901	0.893
2	1.970	1.942	1.913	1.886	1.859	1.833	1.808	1.783	1.759	1.736	1.713	1.690
3	2.941	2.884	2.829	2.775	2.723	2.673	2.624	2.577	2.531	2.487	2.444	2.402
4	3.092	3.808	3.717	3.630	3.546	3.465	3.387	3.312	3.240	3.170	3.102	3.037
5	4.853	4.713	4.580	4.452	4.329	4.212	4.100	3.993	3.890	3.791	3.696	3.605
6	5.795	5.601	5.417	5.242	5.076	4.917	4.767	4.623	4.486	4.355	4.321	4.111
7	6.728	6.472	6.230	6.002	5.786	5.582	5.389	5.206	5.033	4.868	4.712	4.564
8	7.652	7.325	7.020	6.733	6.463	6.210	5.971	5.747	5.535	5.335	5.146	4.968
9	8.566	8.162	7.786	7.435	7.108	6.802	6.515	6.247	5.995	5.759	5.537	5.328
10	9.471	8.983	8.530	8.111	7.722	7.360	7.024	6.710	6.418	6.145	5.889	5.650
11	10.37	9.787	9.253	8.760	8.306	7.887	7.499	7.139	6.805	6.495	6.207	5.938
12	11.26	10.58	9.954	9.385	8.863	8.384	7.943	7.536	7.161	6.814	6.492	6.194
13	12.13	11.35	10.63	9.986	9.394	8.853	8.358	7.904	7.487	7.103	6.750	6.424
14	13.00	12.11	11.30	10.56	9.899	9.295	8.745	8.244	7.786	7.367	6.982	6.628
15	13.87	12.85	11.94	11.12	10.38	9.712	9.108	8.559	8.061	7.606	7.191	6.811
16	14.72	13.58	12.56	11.65	10.84	10.11	9.447	8.851	8.313	7.824	7.379	6.974
17	15.56	14.29	13.17	12.17	11.27	10.48	9.763	9.122	8.544	8.022	7.549	7.120
18	16.40	14.99	13.75	12.66	11.69	10.83	10.06	9.372	8.756	8.201	7.702	7.250
19	17.23	15.68	14.32	13.13	12.09	11.16	10.34	9.604	8.950	8.365	7.839	7.366
20	18.05	16.35	14.88	13.59	12.46	11.47	10.59	9.818	9.129	8.514	7.963	7.469
21	18.86	17.01	15.42	14.03	12.82	11.76	10.84	10.02	9.292	8.649	8.075	7.562
22	19.66	17.66	15.94	14.45	13.16	12.04	11.06	10.20	9.442	8.772	8.176	7.645
23	20.46	18.29	16.44	14.86	13.49	12.30	11.27	10.37	9.580	8.883	8.266	7.718
24	21.24	18.91	16.94	15.25	13.80	12.55	11.47	10.53	9.707	8.985	8.348	7.784
25	22.02	19.52	17.41	15.62	14.09	12.78	11.65	10.67	9.823	9.077	8.422	7.843
26	22.80	20.12	17.88	15.98	14.38	13.00	11.83	10.81	9.929	9.161	8.488	7.896
27	23.56	20.71	18.33	16.33	14.64	13.21	11.99	10.94	10.03	9.237	8.548	7.943
28	24.32	21.28	18.76	16.66	14.90	13.41	12.14	11.05	10.12	9.307	8.602	7.984
29	25.07	21.84	19.19	16.98	15.14	13.59	12.28	11.16	10.20	9.370	8.650	8.022
30	25.81	22.40	19.60	17.29	15.37	13.76	12.41	11.26	10.27	9.427	8.694	8.055

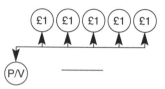

Note: To convert a future cash flow of £1 per period into a present value, apply the factor that matches both the number of years and the interest rate, for example, 6 years, 4 per cent = £5.242

Present value of annuity of £1

Years	13%	14%	15%	16%	17%	18%	19%	20%	21%	22%	23%	24%
1	0.885	0.877	0.870	0.862	0.855	0.847	0.840	0.833	0.826	0.820	0.813	0.806
2	1.668	1.647	1.626	1.605	1.585	1.566	1.547	1.528	1.509	1.492	1.474	1.457
3	2.361	2.322	2.283	2.246	2.210	2.174	2.140	2.106	2.074	2.042	2.011	1.981
4	2.974	2.914	2.855	2.798	2.743	2.690	2.639	2.589	2.540	2.494	2.448	2.404
5	3.517	3.433	3.352	3.274	3.199	3.127	3.058	2.991	2.926	2.864	2.803	2.745
6	3.998	3.889	3.784	3.685	3.589	3.498	3.410	3.326	3.245	3.167	3.092	3.020
7	4.423	4.288	4.160	4.039	3.922	3.812	3.706	3.605	3.508	3.416	3.327	3.242
8	4.799	4.639	4.487	4.344	4.207	4.078	3.954	3.837	3.726	3.619	3.518	3.421
9	5.132	4.946	4.772	4.607	4.451	4.303	4.163	4.031	3.905	3.786	3.673	3.566
10	5.426	5.216	5.019	4.833	4.659	4.494	4.339	4.192	4.054	3.923	3.799	3.682
11	5.687	5.453	5.234	5.029	4.836	4.656	4.486	4.327	4.177	4.035	3.092	3.776
12	5.918	5.660	5.421	5.197	4.988	4.793	4.611	4.439	4.278	4.127	3.985	3.851
13	6.122	5.842	5.583	5.342	5.118	4.910	4.715	4.533	4.362	4.203	4.053	3.912
14	6.302	6.002	5.724	5.468	5.229	5.008	4.802	4.611	4.432	4.265	4.108	3.962
15	6.462	6.142	5.847	5.575	5.324	5.092	4.876	4.675	4.489	4.315	4.153	4.001
16	6.604	6.265	5.954	5.668	5.405	5.162	4.938	4.730	4.536	4.357	4.189	4.033
17	6.729	6.373	6.047	5.749	5.475	5.222	4.990	4.775	4.576	4.391	4.219	4.059
18	6.840	6.467	6.128	5.818	5.534	5.273	5.033	4.812	4.608	4.419	4.243	4.080
19	6.938	6.550	6.198	5.877	5.584	5.316	5.070	4.843	4.635	4.442	4.263	4.097
20	7.025	6.623	6.259	5.929	5.628	5.353	5.101	4.870	4.657	4.460	4.279	4.110
21	7.102	6.687	6.312	5.973	5.665	5.384	5.127	4.891	4.675	4.476	4.292	4.121
22	7.170	6.743	6.359	6.011	5.696	5.410	5.149	4.909	4.690	4.488	4.302	4.130
23	7.230	6.792	6.399	6.044	5.723	5.432	5.167	4.925	4.703	4.499	4.311	4.137
24	7.283	6.835	6.434	6.073	5.746	5.451	5.182	4.937	4.713	4.507	4.318	4.143
25	7.330	6.873	6.464	6.097	5.766	5.467	5.195	4.948	4.721	4.514	4.323	4.147
26	7.372	6.906	6.491	6.118	5.783	5.480	5.206	4.956	4.728	4.520	4.328	4.151
27	7.409	6.935	6.514	6.136	5.798	5.492	5.215	4.964	4.734	4.524	4.332	4.154
28	7.441	6.961	6.534	6.152	5.810	5.502	5.223	4.970	4.739	4.528	4.335	4.157
29	7.470	6.983	6.551	6.166	5.820	5.510	5.229	4.975	4.743	4.531	4.337	4.159
30	7.496	7.003	6.566	6.177	5.829	5.517	5.235	4.979	4.746	4.534	4.339	4.160

Future value of £1

Years	1%	2%	3%	4%	5%	6%	7%	8%	9%	10%	11%	12%
1	1.010	1.020	1.030	1.040	1.050	1.060	1.070	1.080	1.090	1.100	1.110	1.120
2	1.020	1.040	1.061	1.082	1.103	1.124	1.145	1.166	1.188	1.210	1.232	1.254
3	1.030	1.061	1.093	1.125	1.158	1.191	1.225	1.260	1.295	1.331	1.368	1.405
4	1.041	1.082	1.126	1.170	1.216	1.262	1.311	1.360	1.412	1.464	1.518	1.574
5	1.051	1.104	1.159	1.217	1.276	1.338	1.403	1.469	1.539	1.611	1.685	1.762
6	1.062	1.126	1.194	1.265	1.340	1.419	1.501	1.587	1.677	1.772	1.870	1.974
7	1.072	1.149	1.230	1.316	1.407	1.504	1.606	1.714	1.828	1.949	2.076	2.211
8	1.083	1.172	1.267	1.369	1.477	1.594	1.718	1.851	1.993	2.144	2.305	2.476
9	1.094	1.195	1.305	1.423	1.551	1.689	1.838	1.999	2.172	2.358	2.558	2.773
10	1.105	1.219	1.344	1.480	1.629	1.791	1.967	2.159	2.367	2.594	2.839	3.106
11	1.116	1.243	1.384	1.539	1.710	1.898	2.105	2.332	2.580	2.853	3.152	3.479
12	1.127	1.268	1.426	1.601	1.796	2.012	2.252	2.518	2.813	3.138	3.498	3.896
13	1.138	1.294	1.469	1.665	1.886	2.133	2.410	2.720	3.066	3.452	3.883	4.363
14	1.149	1.319	1.513	1.732	1.980	2.261	2.579	2.937	3.342	3.797	4.310	4.887
15	1.161	1.346	1.558	1.801	2.079	2.397	2.759	3.172	3.642	4.177	4.785	5.474
16	1.173	1.373	1.605	1.873	2.183	2.540	2.952	3.426	3.970	4.595	5.311	6.130
17	1.184	1.400	1.653	1.948	2.292	2.693	3.159	3.700	4.328	5.054	5.895	6.866
18	1.196	1.428	1.702	2.026	2.407	2.854	3.380	3.996	4.717	5.560	6.544	7.690
19	1.208	1.457	1.754	2.107	2.527	3.026	3.617	4.316	5.142	6.116	7.263	8.613
20	1.220	1.486	1.806	2.191	2.653	3.207	3.870	4.661	5.604	6.727	8.062	9.646
21	1.232	1.516	1.860	2.279	2.786	3.400	4.141	5.034	6.109	7.400	8.949	10.80
22	1.245	1.546	1.916	2.370	2.925	3.604	4.430	5.437	6.659	8.140	9.934	12.10
23	1.257	1.577	1.974	2.465	3.072	3.820	4.741	5.871	7.258	8.954	11.03	13.55
24	1.270	1.608	2.033	2.563	3.225	4.049	5.072	6.341	7.911	9.850	12.24	15.18
25	1.282	1.641	2.094	2.666	3.386	4.292	5.427	6.848	8.623	10.83	13.59	17.00
26	1.295	1.673	2.157	2.772	3.556	4.549	5.807	7.396	9.399	11.92	15.08	19.04
27	1.308	1.707	2.221	2.883	3.733	4.822	6.214	7.988	10.25	13.11	16.74	21.32
28	1.321	1.741	2.288	2.999	3.920	5.112	6.649	8.627	11.17	14.42	18.58	23.88
29	1.335	1.776	2.357	3.119	4.116	5.418	7.114	9.317	12.17	15.86	20.62	26.72
30	1.348	1.811	2.427	3.243	4.322	5.743	7.612	10.06	13.27	17.45	22.89	29.96

Note: To convert £1 today into a future value apply the factor that matches both the number of years and the interest rate, for example, 6 years, 4 per cent = £1.265.

Future value of £1

Years	13%	14%	15%	16%	17%	18%	19%	20%	21%	22%	23%	24%
1	1.130	1.140	1.150	1.160	1.170	1.180	1.190	1.200	1.210	1.220	1.230	1.240
2	1.277	1.300	1.322	1.346	1.369	1.392	1.416	1.440	1.464	1.488	1.513	1.538
3	1.443	1.482	1.521	1.561	1.602	1.643	1.685	1.728	1.772	1.816	1.861	1.907
4	1.63	1.689	1.749	1.811	1.874	1.939	2.005	2.074	2.144	2.215	2.289	2.364
5	1.842	1.925	2.011	2.100	2.192	2.288	2.386	2.488	2.594	2.703	2.815	2.932
6	2.082	2.195	2.313	2.436	2.565	2.700	2.840	2.986	3.138	3.297	3.463	3.635
7	2.353	2.502	2.660	2.826	3.001	3.185	3.379	3.583	3.797	4.023	4.259	4.508
8	2.658	2.853	3.059	3.278	3.511	3.759	4.021	4.300	4.595	4.908	5.239	5.590
9	3.004	3.252	3.518	3.803	4.108	4.435	4.785	5.160	5.560	5.987	6.444	6.931
10	3.395	3.707	4.046	4.411	4.807	5.234	5.695	6.192	6.727	7.305	7.926	8.594
11	3.836	4.226	4.652	5.117	5.624	6.176	6.777	7.430	8.140	8.912	9.749	10.66
12	4.335	4.818	5.350	5.936	6.580	7.288	8.064	8.916	9.850	10.87	11.99	13.21
13	4.898	5.492	6.153	6.886	7.699	8.599	9.596	10.70	11.92	13.26	14.75	16.39
14	5.535	6.261	7.076	7.988	9.007	10.15	11.42	12.84	14.42	16.18	18.14	20.32
15	6.254	7.138	8.137	9.266	10.54	11.97	13.59	15.41	17.45	19.74	22.31	25.20
16	7.067	8.137	9.358	10.75	12.33	14.13	16.17	18.49	21.11	24.09	27.45	31.24
17	7.986	9.276	10.76	12.47	14.43	16.67	19.24	22.19	25.55	29.38	33.76	38.74
18	9.024	10.58	12.38	14.46	16.88	19.67	22.90	26.62	30.91	35.85	41.52	48.04
19	10.20	12.06	14.23	16.78	19.75	23.21	27.25	31.95	37.40	43.74	51.07	59.57
20	11.52	13.74	16.37	19.46	23.11	27.39	32.43	38.34	45.26	53.36	62.82	73.86
21	13.02	15.67	18.82	22.57	27.03	32.32	38.59	46.01	54.76	65.10	77.27	91.59
22	14.71	17.86	21.64	26.19	31.63	38.14	45.92	55.21	66.26	79.42	95.04	113.6
23	16.63	20.36	24.89	30.38	37.01	45.01	54.65	66.25	80.18	96.89	116.9	140.8
24	18.79	23.21	28.63	35.24	43.30	53.11	65.03	79.50	97.02	118.2	143.8	174.6
25	21.23	26.46	32.92	40.87	50.66	62.67	77.39	95.40	117.4	144.2	176.9	216.5
26	23.99	30.17	37.86	47.41	59.27	73.95	92.09	114.5	142.0	175.9	217.5	268.5
27	27.11	34.39	43.54	55.00	69.35	87.26	109.6	137.4	171.9	214.6	267.6	333.0
28	30.63	39.20	50.07	63.80	81.13	103.0	130.4	164.8	208.0	261.9	329.1	412.9
29	34.62	44.69	57.58	74.01	94.93	121.5	155.2	197.8	251.6	319.5	404.8	512.0
30	39.12	50.95	66.21	85.85	111.1	143.4	184.7	237.4	304.5	389.8	497.9	634.8

Future value of annuity of £1

Years	1%	2%	3%	4%	5%	6%	7%	8%	9%	10%	11%	12%
1	1.000	1.000	1.000	1.000	1.000	1.000	1.000	1.000	1.000	1.000	1.000	1.000
2	2.010	2.020	2.030	2.040	2.050	2.060	2.070	2.080	2.090	2.100	2.110	2.120
3	3.030	3.060	3.091	3.122	3.152	3.184	3.215	3.246	3.278	3.310	3.342	3.374
4	4.060	4.122	4.184	4.246	4.310	4.375	4.440	4.506	4.573	4.641	4.710	4.779
5	5.101	5.204	5.309	5.416	5.526	5.637	5.751	5.867	5.985	6.105	6.228	6.353
6	6.152	6.308	6.468	6.633	6.802	6.975	7.153	7.336	7.523	7.716	7.913	8.115
7	7.214	7.434	7.662	7.898	8.142	8.394	8.654	8.923	9.200	9.487	9.783	10.09
8	8.286	8.583	8.892	9.214	9.549	9.897	10.26	10.64	11.03	11.44	11.86	12.30
9	9.369	9.755	10.16	10.58	11.03	11.49	11.98	12.49	13.02	13.58	14.16	14.78
10	10.46	10.95	11.46	12.01	12.58	13.18	13.82	14.49	15.19	15.94	16.72	17.55
11	11.57	12.17	12.81	13.49	14.21	14.97	15.78	16.65	17.56	18.53	19.56	20.65
12	12.68	13.41	14.19	15.03	15.92	16.87	17.89	18.98	20.14	21.38	22.71	24.13
13	13.81	14.68	15.62	16.63	17.71	18.88	20.14	21.50	22.95	24.52	26.21	28.03
14	14.95	15.97	17.09	18.29	19.60	21.02	22.55	24.21	26.02	27.97	30.09	32.39
15	16.10	17.29	18.60	20.02	21.58	23.28	25.13	27.15	29.36	31.77	34.41	37.28
16	17.26	18.64	20.16	21.82	23.66	25.67	27.89	30.32	33.00	35.95	39.19	42.75
17	18.43	20.01	21.76	23.70	25.84	28.21	30.84	33.75	36.97	40.54	44.50	48.88
18	19.61	21.41	23.41	25.65	28.13	30.91	34.00	37.45	41.30	45.60	50.40	55.75
19	20.81	22.84	25.12	27.67	30.54	33.76	37.38	41.45	46.02	51.16	56.94	63.44
20	22.02	24.30	26.87	29.78	33.07	36.79	41.00	45.76	51.16	57.27	64.20	72.05
21	23.24	25.78	28.68	31.97	35.72	39.99	44.87	50.42	56.76	64.00	72.27	81.70
22	24.47	27.30	30.54	34.25	38.51	43.39	49.01	55.46	62.87	71.40	81.21	92.50
23	25.72	28.84	32.45	36.62	41.43	47.00	53.44	60.89	69.53	79.54	91.15	104.6
24	26.97	30.42	34.43	39.08	44.50	50.82	58.18	66.76	76.79	88.50	102.2	118.2
25	28.24	32.03	36.46	41.65	47.73	54.86	63.25	73.11	84.70	98.35	114.4	133.3
26	29.53	33.67	38.55	44.31	51.11	59.16	68.68	79.95	93.32	109.2	128.0	150.3
27	30.82	35.34	40.71	47.08	54.67	63.71	74.48	87.35	102.7	121.1	143.1	169.4
28	32.13	37.05	42.93	49.97	58.40	68.53	80.70	95.34	113.0	134.2	159.8	190.7
29	33.45	38.79	45.22	52.97	62.32	73.64	87.35	104.0	124.1	148.6	178.4	214.6
30	34.78	40.57	47.58	56.08	66.44	79.06	94.46	113.3	136.3	164.5	199.0	241.3

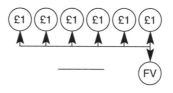

Note: To convert a cash flow of £1 per period into its equivalent 'future value' at the end of the period, apply the factor that matches both the number of years and the interest rate, for example, 6 years, 4 per cent = £6.633

Future value of annuity of £1

Years	13%	14%	15%	16%	17%	18%	19%	20%	21%	22%	23%	24%
1	1.000	1.000	1.000	1.000	1.000	1.000	1.000	1.000	1.000	1.000	1.000	1.000
2	2.130	2.140	2.150	2.160	2.170	2.180	2.190	2.200	2.210	2.220	2.230	2.240
3	3.407	3.440	3.472	3.506	3.539	3.572	3.606	3.640	3.674	3.708	3.743	3.778
4	4.850	4.921	4.993	5.066	5.141	5.215	5.291	5.368	5.446	5.524	5.604	5.684
5	6.480	6.610	6.742	6.877	7.014	7.154	7.297	7.442	7.589	7.740	7.893	8.048
6	8.323	8.536	8.754	8.977	9.207	9.442	9.683	9.930	10.18	10.44	10.71	10.98
7	10.40	10.73	11.07	11.41	11.77	12.14	12.52	12.92	13.32	13.74	14.17	14.62
8	12.76	13.23	13.73	14.24	14.77	15.33	15.90	16.50	17.12	17.76	18.43	19.12
9	15.42	16.09	16.79	17.52	18.28	19.09	19.92	20.80	21.71	22.67	23.67	24.71
10	18.42	19.34	20.30	21.32	22.39	23.52	24.71	25.96	27.27	28.66	30.11	31.64
11	21.81	23.04	24.35	25.73	27.20	28.76	30.40	32.15	34.00	35.96	38.04	40.24
12	25.65	27.27	29.00	30.85	32.82	34.93	37.18	39.58	42.14	44.87	47.79	50.89
13	29.98	32.09	34.35	36.79	39.40	42.22	45.24	48.50	51.99	55.75	59.78	64.11
14	34.88	37.58	40.50	43.67	47.10	50.82	54.84	59.20	63.91	69.01	74.53	80.50
15	40.42	43.84	47.58	51.66	56.11	60.97	66.26	72.04	78.33	85.19	92.67	100.8
16	46.67	50.98	55.72	60.93	66.65	72.94	79.85	87.44	95.78	104.9	115.0	126.0
17	53.74	59.12	65.08	71.67	78.98	87.07	96.02	105.9	116.9	129.0	142.4	157.3
18	61.73	68.39	75.84	84.14	93.41	103.7	115.3	128.1	142.4	158.4	176.2	196.0
19	70.75	78.97	88.21	98.60	110.3	123.4	138.2	154.7	173.4	194.3	217.7	244.0
20	80.95	91.02	102.4	115.4	130.0	146.6	165.4	186.7	210.8	238.0	268.8	303.6
21	92.47	104.8	118.8	134.8	153.1	174.0	197.8	225.0	256.0	291.3	331.6	377.5
22	105.5	120.4	137.6	157.4	180.2	206.3	236.4	271.0	310.8	356.4	408.9	469.1
23	120.2	138.3	159.3	183.6	211.8	244.5	282.4	326.2	377.0	435.9	503.9	582.9
24	136.8	158.7	184.2	214.0	248.8	289.5	337.0	392.5	457.2	532.8	620.8	723.5
25	155.6	181.9	212.8	249.2	292.1	342.6	402.0	472.0	554.2	651.0	764.6	898.1
26	176.9	208.3	245.7	290.1	342.8	405.3	479.4	567.4	671.6	795.2	941.5	1115
27	200.8	238.5	283.6	337.5	402.0	479.2	571.5	681.9	813.7	971.1	1159	1383
28	227.9	272.9	327.1	392.5	471.4	566.5	681.1	819.2	985.5	1186	1427	1716
29	258.6	312.1	377.2	456.3	552.5	669.4	811.5	984.1	1194	1448	1756	2129
30	293.2	356.8	434.7	530.3	647.4	790.9	966.7	1182	1445	1767	2160	2641

GLOSSARY

All items in *italics* are defined elsewhere in the glossary

Acid test *see quick ratio*

Activity ratios These measure the relationship between key assets and sales. They express how well assets are being utilised. For instance, 'accounts receivable days' (*see debtor days*) shows how long cash is tied up in accounts receivable; likewise *inventory days*. We use the *sales to fixed assets ratio* to give a measure of the output being generated by major fixed assets. The term 'asset utilisation ratios' is also used in this context.

Amortisation of loan The repayment of a loan by equal periodic payments that include both interest on outstanding balance plus some repayment of principal.

Annuity A series of equal payments made at equal intervals of time. Many financial calculations can be treated by the annuity formulae, for example repayment of a term loan, straight line depreciation charges, and so on.

Arbitrage The operation of buying and selling a security simultaneously in two different markets to take advantage of inconsistencies in pricing.

Asset backing Also known as 'asset value per share', it is calculated by dividing total ordinary funds in the balance sheet by the number of issued ordinary shares.

Asset utilisation ratios *See activity ratios.*

Asset value per share *See asset backing.*

Authorised share capital The maximum value of share capital that can be issued. It is specified in the company Articles and can be increased only by permission of the shareholders.

Average collection period As *debtor days*.

Average interest rate paid The apparent rate of interest paid on loans, calculated by expressing the interest charge in the profit and loss account as a percentage of loan funds in the balance sheet. It must be kept in mind that loans at the balance sheet date may not be a true reflection of the average over the year.

Bear Term for an investor who anticipates a falling market in financial securities. This investor may sell securities not owned in order to profit from the expected drop in price. *See* also *bull*.

Beta value A measure of the risk in a share that cannot be eliminated by diversification. High risk brings the need for a high return. Therefore the beta value is used by analysts to derive an appropriate share value.

Blue chip A first-class commercial security.

Bond US term for medium- to long-term loan. Legally it is the certificate that gives the holder the right to periodic interest payments and repayment of principal.

Bonus issue New equity shares issued from reserves and given free to company shareholders in proportion to their existing share holdings.

Book value per share The value of a share based on the balance sheet values. *See* also *asset backing*.

Borrowing ratio Long-term plus short-term loans expressed as a percentage of ordinary funds plus preference shares less intangibles.

Break-even point The level of activity at which the fixed costs of an operation are just covered by the contribution from sales. At this point neither a profit nor a loss ensues.

Break-even analysis A form of analysis that relates activity to totals of revenue and costs based on the classification of costs into fixed and variable types.

Bull An investor who anticipates a rise in the price level of financial securities. This investor may purchase securities with the intention of resale before the time for settlement is due. *See* also *bear.*

Bullet A single payment of the total amount of a loan at the end of the period (as opposed to periodic payments during its life).

Capital asset pricing model (CAPM) A model that links risk and return for all types of security. Applied to the valuation of equity shares, it uses the risk coefficient (*beta value*) of the share to calculate the required risk premium. This risk premium is added to the risk-free rate (rate on *gilts*) to give the appropriate yield for the share.

Call The amount demanded from shareholders from the balance outstanding on non-paid-up shares.

Call option An option to purchase. *See* also *option.*

Capital employed The total of the long-term funds in the balance sheet. It includes shareholders' funds, long-term loans, preference shares, minority interests and miscellaneous long-term funds. It can also be expressed as total assets less current liabilities.

Capital market The financial market for long-term securities.

Capital project appraisal Evaluation of expenditure on capital assets to establish its rate of return with a view to deciding on whether or not to make the investment.

Capital reserves Shareholders' funds that have originated from sources other than trading or the nominal value of new issues.

Capital structure The mix of financing in a company. It usually refers to the proportions of debt and equity in the balance sheet.

Cash cycle A model of working capital cash flow that identifies the time required for cash paid out for raw materials and expenses to come back in from accounts receivable.

Cash flow, incremental The extra cash in-flow or out-flow that comes from selecting one alternative over another in capital project appraisal.

Cash flow per share Profit after interest, tax, minority and preference dividends plus depreciation divided by the number of shares.

Caveat emptor 'Let the buyer beware' – an expression that emphasises the duty of a party to a contract to ensure that its interests are protected.

Certificate of deposit (CD) A short-term negotiable certificate issued by a bank as evidence of a deposit that is repayable on a fixed date. It is a highly liquid bearer instrument.

Collateral A physical or financial asset used as security for a loan.

Commercial paper Loan notes issued by high-credit corporations to raise short-term funds direct from the money markets rather than from a lending institution.

Common size financial statements Statements that have been standardised by having each component expressed as a percentage of sales or total assets.

Compensating balance The minimum amount by which a company must stay in credit on a deposit account under the terms of a loan.

Consols UK Government stock secured on the Consolidated Fund. They are effectively non-redeemable loans to the government with a low nominal interest rate.

Constant growth model A valuation model, derived by Professor Gordon, that calculates a share value from its dividend flow to infinity under assumptions of constant growth.

Contingent liability A potential liability that may not arise but which must be mentioned in the notes to the published accounts of a company.

Conversion ratio The number of shares the holder of a convertible security receives for each bond on conversion.

Convertible Loan A loan that gives the lender the option to convert into shares at a fixed price for a period of time.

Cost of capital The weighted average cost of funds to a company, based on the mix of equity and loan capital and their respective costs. A distinction is usually drawn between the average cost of all funds in an existing balance sheet and the marginal cost of raising new funds.

Covenant, restrictive A clause in a loan agreement to restrict the freedom of the borrower to act in a way that would weaken the position of the lender, such as increasing the amount of the dividend.

Credit period The number of days' sales represented by the accounts receivable. It corresponds with the term *debtor days*.

Current assets The sum of inventories, accounts receivable, cash and cash equivalents and miscellaneous short-term assets.

Current liabilities The sum of accounts payable, short-term loans and miscellaneous accruals all due for repayment within one year.

Debenture A legal document that acknowledges a loan. In the US, the term refers to an unsecured loan. In the UK it may be secured by a fixed or floating charge on the assets.

Debtor days, or, accounts receivable days The figure for trade debtors in the balance sheet is divided by the average sales per day to express the average number of days' credit taken by customers.

Debt to equity ratio The principal measure of the mix of funds in a company's balance sheet. It can be expressed in a number of different ways. The most common way is to calculate the percentage that total interest bearing debt bears to ordinary plus preference shareholders' funds.

Debt to total assets ratio One of the debt to equity measures. Long term loans plus current liabilities are expressed as a percentage of total assets.

Deferred tax A taxation amount that has been charged to the profit and loss account but which has not been paid over to the authorities and is not currently payable. Timing differences between accounting and taxation computations of taxable profit on account of depreciation and so on are the root cause.

Departmental ratios The effectiveness of the major departments can be assessed by using an approach similar to that for the total operation, as illustrated in Chapter 7. For each department, costs and assets classified under selected headings are related to sales, cost of sales or standard hours of work produced as

appropriate. Suggested ratios for Marketing and Production are shown below:
- Marketing: cost to sales ratios
  salaries and commission
  travel expenses
  advertising costs
  sales office costs
- Marketing: assets to sales ratios
  fixed assets: office
  fixed assets: cars/equipment
  finished goods
  accounts receivable
- Production: cost to cost of sales ratios
  direct material
  direct labour
  overtime
  indirect labour
  maintenance
  production planning
  supervision and so on
- Production: asset to cost of sales ratios
  fixed assets: factory premises
  fixed assets: plant
  fixed assets: vehicles
  raw material
  work in progress.

Dilution　The reduction in the *earnings per share* value due to an increase in the number of shares issued or contracted to be issued in the future.

Discounted cash flow (DCF)　A method of appraisal for investment projects. The total incremental stream of cash from a project is tested to assess the return it delivers to the investor. If the return exceeds the required, or, *hurdle rate*, the project is recommended on financial terms and vice versa. Two approaches can be used in the assessment: *see net present value (NPV)* and *internal rate of return (IRR)*.

Discounting　A technique used to calculate the present value of a cash flow occurring in some future time period. It is used in connection with the sale for immediate cash of a future debt and, more extensively, in translating future cash flow from an investment into present values.

Dividend cover　Expresses the number of times that dividends to the ordinary shareholders are covered by earnings. *See* also *payout ratio*.

Dividend per share (DPS)　The actual dividend paid on each ordinary share. It can be calculated from the accounts by dividing the total ordinary dividend by the number of ordinary shares.

Dividend yield　Actual dividend per share expressed as a percentage of the current share price. In the UK, imputed tax is added to dividends paid and the calculation gives gross dividend yield.

Earnings per share (EPS)　The profit earned for the ordinary shareholders as shown in the profit and loss account is divided by the number of issued ordinary shares to give earnings per share. (To be strictly orthodox the weighted average number of share should be used) Under the UK system of imputation tax three methods of calculating earnings can be used. These are referred to as 'nil', 'net', 'max'. The 'nil' method assumes no distribution of dividend. The 'net' method adjusts for unrelievable advance corporation tax (ACT). The 'max' method adds back the maximum amount of ACT that could be recovered if all profits were distributed. (See 'A Guide to Financial Times Statistics' from Financial Times Business Information.)

Earnings yield (K) Earnings per share expressed as a percentage of the current share price. In the UK, imputed tax is added to earnings to give gross yield.

Employee ratios To measure the productivity of labour, three major variables – sales, profits and assets – are related back to the number of employees and their remuneration. The principal ratios used are:
- remuneration to employee
- sales to employee
- sales to remuneration
- profit to employee
- profit to remuneration
- fixed assets to employee
- working capital to employee.

Equity gearing Ordinary funds plus preference shares expressed as percentage of long-term loan plus current liabilities.

Eurodollar Deposits denominated in US dollars in a bank outside the US owned by a non-resident of the US.

Extraordinary item A significant transaction outside the normal activities of the business and likely to be non-recurring. An example would be the sale of the corporate head office at a large profit. There is a strong argument that such a transaction should not be allowed to distort the trading results and that it should be isolated from the reported earnings. However, the contrary argument that all such gains and losses should be included in the profit and loss account now prevails.

Factoring A method of raising funds by the selling of trade debtors.

Fixed cost A type of cost where the total expenditure does not vary with the level of activity or output.

Fixed assets Land and buildings, plant and equipment and other long-term physical assets on which the operations of the company depends.

Floating rate note (FRN) Loan on which the interest rate varies with prevailing short-term market rates.

Forward cover The purchase or sale of foreign currency for delivery at a fixed future time. It is used to cover against the risk of an adverse exchange rate movement.

Forward exchange rate A rate fixed to govern the exchange of currencies at a fixed future date.

Free borrowing percentage The percentage of non-equity funds that is made up of 'free' debt, that is accounts payable, accruals and deferred tax.

Futures contract A contract in an organised exchange to trade in a fixed quantity of a security at a fixed price at a future date.

Gearing A relationship between different types of funds in a company, such as loans and equity. The higher the amount of loan funds the higher the amount of fixed interest charge in the profit and loss account. Where interest charges are high, a small change in operating profit will have a much increased result in return to the equity for shareholders.

Gilts The term 'gilt-edged' refers to British government longer term borrowing instruments. They are described as 'short' where the maturity is up to five years, 'medium' for periods of five to 15 years and 'long' for over 15 years to infinity.

Hedging A technique for reducing the risk of an exposed position by taking a compensating position in another security.

Hurdle rate The rate of return decided on by a company as the minimum acceptable for capital investment. It will be governed by the firms' cost of capital and it may allow for different levels of risk.

Intangible assets Long-term non-physical assets in the balance sheet such as goodwill and brand values.

Interest cover A liquidity ratio that expresses the number of times the interest charged in the profit and loss account is covered by profit before interest and tax.

Internal rate of return (IRR) The rate of discount that brings the present value of all the cash flows associated with a capital investment to zero. It measures the effective yield on the investment. If this yield is greater than the 'hurdle rate' the investment is deemed to be financially desirable and vice versa.

Inventory days The inventory value in the balance sheet is expressed in terms of days. The divisor is usually the average daily cost of sales. Separate calculations are made for raw materials, work in progress and finished goods.

Investments Investments in subsidiary and associated companies and other long-term financial assets.

Junk bonds High-interest-bearing bonds with little security of assets issued by a company with good cash flow.

LIBOR London Interbank Offered Rate - the rate at which major banks in the short-term money market lend to each other. It is a benchmark for many international loans and floating-rate issues to corporations

Lease – finance A lease under which the lessee assumes all the risks and rewards of ownership. It extends over the estimated economic life of the assets and cannot easily be cancelled. Under current accounting rules, such a lease is treated as a loan.

Leverage *See gearing.*

Leveraged buy-out The acquisition of a firm by using large amounts of debt.

Liquidity The ability to provide cash to meet day-to-day needs as they arise.

Long-term loans (LTL) Bank and other loans of more than one year.

Market to book ratio The relationship between the balance sheet value of the ordinary shares and their market value. The expression 'price to book' is also used.

Market capitalisation The notional total market value of a company calculated from the latest quoted market price of the share multiplied by the number of shares. The quoted price may not give an accurate value for the total shares, it may refer to only one small block of shares.

Market value weights In cost of capital calculations, the weighted cost can be derived using either the book value or market value weights to determine the overall weighted cost.

Matching principle A rule that a firm should match short-term uses of funds with short-term sources and long-term uses with long-term sources.

Minority interests The book value of shares in a subsidiary that are owned by members who are not shareholders of the parent company.

Miscellaneous current assets Sundry receivables and pre-payments due for realisation within one year.

Miscellaneous long-term funds A composite entry in the balance sheet that may include deferred tax, unamortised government grants, provision for pensions and so on.

Money market A term applied to the trading in short-term financial instruments in London.

Mutually exclusive projects In an investment appraisal exercise these are projects that compete with one another so that the acceptance of one means the exclusion of the others.

Net working capital *See working capital.*

Net worth (NW) The sum of issued ordinary shares plus all reserves plus preference shares less intangibles assets.

Net present value (NPV) A positive or negative value arrived at by discounting the cash flow from a capital project by the desired rate of return. If the value is positive, it means that the project is financially desirable and vice versa.

Off-balance sheet A term that refers to borrowing that does not appear on the balance sheet. Sometimes achieved by a finance lease that gives the lessee all the risks and rewards, but not the legal status, of ownership.

Opportunity cost The alternative advantage foregone as a result of the commitment of resources to one particular end.

Optimal capital structure The point at which the cost of capital to a company is reduced to the minimum by the best mix of debt and equity.

Option A financial instrument that gives the holder the right, but not the obligation, to purchase or sell a specified asset at a specified price on or before a set date. *See put option; call option.*

Ordinary funds (OF) The sum of the issued ordinary shares, capital reserves and revenue reserves. The total represents the assets remaining to the ordinary shareholders after all prior claims have been satisfied.

Over the counter (OTC) Refers to the market where shares and financial instruments are traded outside the formal exchanges.

Overtrading A company is in an overtrading situation when there is not sufficient *liquidity* to meet comfortably the day-to-day cash needs of the existing level of business. There is constant danger of bankruptcy, even though the company may be trading profitably. Such a situation can come about because of past trading losses, excessive expansion and so on, but can be cured by the injection of long-term funds or, maybe, the sale of fixed assets.

Paid borrowing percentage The percentage of non-equity funds consisting of interest-bearing debt.

Par value A notional value assigned to a share largely for accounting purposes.

Payback period A term used in investment appraisal. It refers to the time required for the non-discounted cash in-flow to accumulate to the initial cash out-flow in the investment.

Payout ratio The percentage of earnings available for distribution that is paid out in dividends. This ratio is the reciprocal of *dividend cover*.

Preference capital Shares that have preferential rights over ordinary shares. These rights normally relate to distribution of dividends and repayment of capital. The shares usually carry a fixed dividend but also carry very little voting power.

Preferred creditors Creditors who, in an insolvency, have a statutory right to be paid in full before any other claims. Employees who have pay due to them would normally be in this category.

Present value (P/V) A sum calculated by discounting the stream of future cash flow from a project using an interest rate equal to the desired rate of return. It differs from *net present value* in that the amount of the investment is not included in the cash flows.

Price to earnings multiple (PE) The value derived by dividing the current share price by the *earnings per share*. Latest reported earnings or prospective earnings for the coming year may be used in the calculation.

Prime rate The rate at which banks lend to corporations with the highest credit ratings.

Profitability index A measure for assessing the relative merit of an investment by expressing the present value of the future cash flows as a percentage of the investment amount.

Profit after tax (PAT) Profit available for the shareholders after interest and tax has been deducted.

Profit before interest, tax and depreciation (PBITD) This value corresponds very closely to cash flow from trading.

Profit before interest and tax (PBIT) Operating profit plus other income.

Profit before tax (PBT) Operating profit plus other income less total interest charged.

Profit for ordinary (PFO) The after-tax profit in the profit and loss account from which preference and minority dividends have been deducted.

Pro forma statements Projected financial statements

Proxy vote Vote cast by an authorised person on behalf of another.

Put option An option to sell. *See* also *option*.

Quick ratio (acid test) A short-term liquidity ratio calculated by dividing current assets less inventories by current liabilities.

Retained earnings (RE) The final figure from the profit and loss account that is transferred to reserves in the balance sheet.

Repurchase agreement (REPO) A technique for providing short-term cash to a borrower who agrees to sell a security at one price and buy it back at a slightly higher price in the future. The price difference is the effective interest payment to the lender.

Return on capital This is profit before tax but after interest as a percentage of capital employed.

Revenue reserves Increases in shareholders' funds that have arisen from retained profits and are available for distribution as dividends.

Rights issue A new issue of shares made by a company to its existing shareholders at a price below the current market value.

Risk-free rate of interest The yield available on government *gilts*.

Return on assets (ROA) Profit before interest and tax as percentage of total assets. The corresponding term used in this book is return on total assets.

Return on capital employed (ROCE) Capital employed includes all the long-term funds in the balance sheet, that is shareholders' funds plus long-term loan plus miscellaneous long-term funds. Profit before tax is often expressed as a percentage of this to give return on capital employed. However, as the denominator includes long-term loan, the corresponding interest on these loans should be added back into the numerator.

Return on equity (ROE) A measure of the percentage return generated by a company for the equity shareholders. It is calculated by expressing profit after tax as a percentage of shareholders' funds. (Where preference shares exist, they should first be deducted from shareholders' funds and the preference dividends also be deducted from the profit figure.)

Return on investment (ROI) A term that is very widely used in connection with the performance of a company or project. It is calculated in many different ways. Usually a pre-tax profit figure is expressed as a percentage of either the long-term funds or the total funds in the balance sheet.

Return on total assets (ROTA) Profit before interest and tax expressed as a percentage of total assets.

Sales and leaseback agreement A method of raising finance whereby a firm sells property to the funding agency and simultaneously signs a long-term lease agreement. The company receives an immediate lump sum in exchange for a series of lease payments in the future.

Sales to fixed assets (times) An activity and performance ratio, calculated by dividing the net fixed assets value in the balance sheet into the sales turnover figure.

Senior debt Debt that ranks ahead of junior, or, subordinated debt in the event of a liquidation. *See subordinated debt.*

Sensitivity analysis Analysis of the change in the output values of an equation from small changes in input values. It is used to assess the risk in an investment project.

Share premium The difference between a share's nominal value and its sale price.

Shareholders' funds Issued ordinary shares plus reserves plus preference shares.

Spontaneous financing Short-term financing that automatically results from the normal operations of the business. Creditors/accounts payable and certain accruals are the main sources.

Short-term loans (STL) The bank overdraft, current portion of long-term debt and other interest-bearing liabilities due within one year.

Subordinated debt Debt that ranks for repayment after *senior debt.*

Subsidiaries A company is a subsidiary of another if the other owns more than 50 per cent of the equity or effectively controls the company by means of voting shares or composition of the board of directors.

Sundry accruals An entry in the current liabilities section of the balance sheet that includes sundry accounts payable plus accrued dividends, interest, tax plus other accruals.

SWAP The exchange of debt and/or currency obligations between parties to their mutual benefit. The benefit can arise from their differing needs for currency and/or fixed/floating interest charges.

Tangible assets The total of all assets in the balance sheet less intangibles, such as goodwill.

Tax rate The apparent rate of tax on profit found by expressing tax charged in the accounts as a percentage of profit before tax.

Term loan Usually a medium-term loan (three to seven years) repaid in fixed, periodic instalments that cover both interest and principal over the life of the loan.

Terminal value A notional cash in-flow attributed to a capital project to allow for value remaining in the project at the final year of the assessment.

Total assets The sum of fixed assets plus intangibles plus investments plus current assets.

Treasury stock   Ordinary or common shares that have been repurchased by the company.

Ultra vires   'Beyond authorised powers'. An act is deemed to be *ultra vires* if carried out by an agent or director of a company in excess of their authority. The person who so acts may incur personal liability.

Underwriting   Banks or other financial institutions guarantee to take up an issue of shares at a specific price in order to ensure the success of the issue. This process in called underwriting.

Variable costs   A type of cost where the total expenditure varies in proportion to activity or output.

Weighted average cost of capital (WACC)   *See cost of capital.*

Warrant   Sometimes attached to loan stock as a sweetener at the time of issue, warrants give an option to the holder to purchase a stated amount of equities at a fixed price for a defined period

Weighted average cost of capital   *See cost of capital.*

Window dressing   The alteration of financial statements at the time of publication to give an artificially improved appearance to the company situation. For instance the temporary sale of inventories to a bank with agreement to repurchase could give an enhanced view of company liquidity.

Working capital   The excess of current assets over current liabilities.

Working capital days   The length of the working capital cycle is often calculated as inventories plus accounts receivable less accounts payable days.

Working capital to sales   A liquidity ratio that is calculated by expressing working capital as a percentage of sales.

Z-growth factor   A value that gives an indication of the self-funding growth rate of a company. It is calculated by expressing retained earnings before *extraordinary items* as a percentage of opening ordinary funds. It is assumed for this calculation that all assets are linearly related to sales, likewise all items in the profit and loss account. It also assumes that existing debt to equity ratios will be maintained.

Zero coupon bond   A bond that pays no interest but is issued at a discount on its face value. The redemption of the bond at par ensures the desired yield to the purchaser.

INDEX